The New

Home Office

An Introduction

The New Home Office
An Introduction

Published by
WATERSIDE PRESS
Domum Road
Winchester SO23 9NN
United Kingdom

Telephone 01962 855567 UK Landline low-cost calls 0845 2300 733
E-mail enquiries@watersidepress.co.uk
Online catalogue and bookstore www.watersidepress.co.uk

ISBN 978 1904380 368

Cataloguing-In-Publication Data A catalogue record for this book can be obtained from the British Library

Cover design © 2007 Waterside Press. Photographs of the Home Office and Houses of Parliament commissioned by Waterside Press.

Part of a two book set with *The New Ministry of Justice: An Introduction* (ISBN 978 1904380 351. The ISBN for the two volumes together is 978 1904380 375).

North American distributor International Specialised Book Services (ISBS), 920 NE 58th Ave, Suite 300, Portland, Oregon, 97213-3786, USA Telephone 1 800 944 6190 Fax 1 503 280 8832 orders@isbs.com www.isbs.com

The New

Home Office

An Introduction

Bryan Gibson

With a Foreword by **David Faulkner CB**

WATERSIDE PRESS

Acknowledgements

This book could not have been written without the help of many people too numerous to mention, but I am particularly grateful to various regular Waterside Press authors with whom I have been able to discuss some of its finer points. In the run up to publication, I also had various reasons to be grateful to Peter Williams, Alex Gibson, John Lyon and Bob Morris.

As ever, my thanks are due to Waterside Press house editor, Jane Green.

I am also indebted to David Faulkner of the Centre for Criminal Justice Research at Oxford University for glancing over the manuscript and agreeing to write the Foreword. His knowledge of this aspect of our public institutions and its background goes back over many years and is, I think, quite unrivalled. Some of his own thoughts on the historic remit and responsibilities of the UK Home Office and how it might have been better organized appear in his influential work *Crime, State and Citizen: A Field Full of Folk* by which I have been greatly informed. To an extent, his ideas take on the status of prophecy. In the outcome David offered more support than I had anticipated and I am indebted to him for this. I must stress, however, that the process of writing this book - and its counterpart *The New Ministry of Justice* - took place in a novel context in which not just two but, so it later transpired, several of the UK's major departments of state were being significantly altered. Information, developments and nuances were at times emerging by the day. Any errors that may have resulted from such dynamics remain mine alone.

I must also acknowledge the various sources now available on the internet that I have tried to read, digest and whenever possible reflect upon as they flashed by on my computer screen. Links to some of the more important and useful of these together with other references are noted in *Appendix V*. I would stress, however, that this book is not intended as a detailed or academic work, rather it is no more than is claimed in the sub-title, an introduction – but one in which I have tried to capture something of the security, law and order and enforcement *zeitgeist* that now appears to be roaming free in and around the new Home Office headquarters in Marsham Street, Westminster.

Bryan Gibson
August 2007

The New Home Office

CONTENTS

CHAPTER

About the author

Bryan Gibson grew up in South Yorkshire before moving to Cambridge, Salisbury, Bristol, London, Basingstoke and Winchester during his legal career. He is a barrister, former co-editor of the weekly legal newspaper *Justice of the Peace* and a regular contributor to this and other national media. He founded Waterside Press in 1989 and has since written or edited a number of books for that imprint on aspects of crime and punishment as well as working on a special project to create an *A-Z of Criminal Justice.*

The author of the Foreword

David Faulkner CB was for many years deputy under secretary of state at the Home Office where he worked with no fewer than seven different home secretaries, gaining unique insights into and experience of the workings of central government. He is now a senior research fellow at the Centre for Criminal Justice Research at Oxford University and a prominent and widely respected commentator on constitutional matters. His writings include the acclaimed *Crime State and Citizen: A Field Full of Folk* (Second edition, Waterside Press, 2006).

Foreword David Faulkner

The Home Office has a long and for the most part honourable history. The office of Secretary of State goes back to 1377, but the Home Office itself was formed in 1782 when pressure of work required the Secretary of State's functions to be divided between the Home Department and Foreign Affairs. The home secretary was then responsible for the whole range of domestic (and for a time colonial) policy, but the process of hiving off further subjects to separate departments began with health and education in the 19th century and has continued ever since. The present need for shared departmental responsibility and partnership with regard to some aspects of public life emphasises how difficult it is to place some responsibilities into tidy compartments.

Until quite recently, the Home Office still had a bewildering range of functions, some of them such as the use of the title 'Royal' or the protection of wild birds being quite remote from its main business. But policing, the control of immigration, the criminal law and the treatment of offenders were always the most prominent, the most difficult and the most politically contentious of the Home Secretary's responsibilities.

There were attempts at various times to define and communicate the core values in which the Home Office believed. For much of the 20th century they were expressed in terms such as 'freedom under the law' and the 'liberty of the individual'. The department's task was to maintain the rights and liberty of individuals within the framework of the criminal and civil law, and to act towards them in a generally humane and liberal spirit. On the whole, staff tried to do that, and felt some self-confidence and some pride in the work they were asked to undertake.

Even so, for the Home Office publicly to claim values such as these would by the 1980s have been a matter for derision among some critics who saw the department as institutionally repressive and insensitive, or who considered it to be irresponsibly liberal and feeble in its treatment of various categories of 'undeserving' people, such as foreigners and criminals. In later years and in some people's eyes, the latter sometimes included ministers themselves who ignored underlying values or sought too dispense to readily with longstanding principles. Nor was the office greatly respected in Whitehall itself, where other departments were inclined to see it as old-fashioned, complacent, and slow to adopt new techniques of management or financial controls. With changes of staff and the increasing politicisation of Home Office business from the 1960s onwards, few people would now be conscious of what might termed the 'old' Home Office values, and fewer still would have felt able to identify themselves openly with them.

The 15 years leading up to the creation of the Ministry of Justice (MOJ) in 2007 were an exceptionally turbulent period, especially in terms of the 'politicisation' already noted above, from 1993 onwards. More issues came to be decided as matters of political rather than professional or experienced administrative judgement, and politically driven reforms caused increasing tension between the Home Office, its own operational services and the judiciary (without whose like-minded approach it could not deliver its sentencing policies in the absence of unequivocal and unduly restricting legislation). Ministers became more active in promoting new initiatives and a mass of new legislation, often with what proved to be unrealistic expectations of what they could achieve. The terrorist incidents in 2001 and 2005 added to the pressures on the department, and events in other parts of the world brought increases in immigration and applications for asylum. The department was at the same time trying to manage a prison population which was at crisis level, and to bring about controversial reforms in prisons and probation. The department's difficulty in responding to the demands being made upon it led to the (arguably unjustified) resignation of Charles Clarke as home secretary in 2006, and the decision to split the Home Office in the following year.

The decision to separate responsibility for policing, immigration and security on the one hand from that for criminal law, sentencing and prisons and probation on the other made some sense, both logically and as a matter of principle.[1] There is a similar division in other countries, with both common law and civil law traditions. It should enable ministers to give more concentrated attention to both sets of responsibilities, and their departments to develop greater depths of expertise. Other changes in government may bring greater self-confidence and mutual respect.

Critics may see a danger that 'the new Home Office' will become too single-mindedly a department of internal security, and develop a culture which sees all the issues of policing or immigration as matters of criminal law and law enforcement, one too suspicious of diversity or idiosyncrasy, and too prone to disproportionate responses. It seems especially odd that a department which is focused on subjects which are seen as threatening the nation's stability and security should have responsibility for anti-social behaviour. These are however concerns which can be dealt with by political and professional leadership and by making sure that the Home Office, in its new form, is open, accessible, responsive to its stakeholders and citizens, and that it operates within an effective framework of democratic and Cabinet accountability.

David Faulkner, August 2007

---

1   For some of the arguments in favour of an MOJ, see *Chapter 1* of this work and for further detail its companion volume, *The New Ministry of Justice.*

Preface

An amalgam of four key strands of development concerning United Kingdom public affairs came together in 2007 to justify the epithet 'new Home Office':

- first, the reorganization – or 'shaking out' – that occurred at the 'old Home Office' in May of that year, when several of its former responsibilities were relinquished to a freshly created Ministry of Justice (MOJ);
- second, the leaner, 'slimmed down' variety of Home Office that resulted, free to concentrate on such matters as homeland security, border controls and issues of a public safety/cum/law and order nature;
- third, the advantages that for the Home Office and its many partners flow from an acceleration in scientific advances - such as those in relation to cyber-technology, forensics (especially DNA), data storage and data sharing, surveillance, monitoring, intelligence gathering, risk analysis and assessment and other modern-day tools of the kind described in *Chapter 3*;
- fourth, the new and seemingly more balanced approach to the great debate on crime and punishment – and with regard to terrorism in particular – that has been accompanied latterly by a distinctly changed approach to public pronouncements, following a change of prime minister and the appointment of the UK's first woman home secretary, Jacqui Smith.

No doubt other people will have their own analysis and might wish to include, in particular, the unprecedented build up in criminal justice legislation and maybe prison overcrowding. But the points noted above are sufficiently broad brush to indicate that there has been a watershed or step-change. The strategic role of a changed Home Office in these events is the main focus of this book.

'Not fit for purpose'

Famously, the creation of the MOJ and the giving up to the MOJ by the Home Office of the latter's responsibilities with regard to the National Offender Management Service (NOMS) and Parole Board occurred after the then home secretary, Dr John Reid, stated publicly, earlier in 2007, that the Home Office had become 'not fit for purpose'. Its cumbersome nature and web-like amalgam of departments, groups, units and responsibilities often placed it in the political and media firing line, notably, in modern times, following the London bombings of 7 July 2005 (and similar though unsuccessful terrorist attempts that followed: all in the wake of 11 September 2002). Controversial issues included detention without trial, control orders, the 'foreign prisoner crisis' (whereby foreign prisoners were not being adequately considered for deportation to their own countries after serving their sentences in accordance with prior judicial recommendations), and re-offending by some serious offenders after they were released from prison.

Seemingly, a kind of malaise had set in perhaps spurred on by media criticism, perceptions of less than supportive judges and the constraints of international obligations (including human rights law). Ever since its 17th century origins, the Home Office tended to 'take to itself' anything remotely connected with its key public safety and law and order responsibilities. Hence, ultimately, the mammoth department that Dr Reid inherited and ultimately concluded was impossible to control in its existing form.

Leaner, fitter and more focused

I hope that as well as providing a straightforward outline of the new Home Office, its component parts, responsibilities and main partners, some sense emerges in this book of what has been described by government as a 'leaner, fitter, less distracted and more focused' department of state. *The New Home Office* can be read on its own or usefully alongside a companion volume, *The New Ministry of Justice: An Introduction* that deals with the justice, constitutional and democratic side of this same equation. As with similar books in the Waterside Press introductory range, the aim is to provide a basic, accessible and constructive account that will be as much of interest to newcomers, students and general readers as it will be to seasoned practitioners or researchers seeking a ready-made perspective. The book looks at the remit of the new Home Office, but against a wider backdrop. Where developments are controversial or complicated it may stray beyond this.

A fresh start and a new era

In *Chapter 10*, I have tried to summarise how the changes described across this book might, properly built upon, lay the foundations for an era of progressive reform. This will come at a time of new challenges, democratic renewal (led via the MOJ) and wide scale reform of public services in general. Within this, the Home Office will need to rely on law-abiding citizens and communities, shared values, supportive 'hearts and minds', cross-agency cooperation and, so we learn, a resurgence of Britishness (*Chapters 2* and *10*). But we cannot return to the mythical golden age of *Dixon of Dock Green*. Organized crime, terrorism, the internet, globalisation and the faster pace of life have put an end to that. As incoming prime minister, Gordon Brown, has proclaimed:

> The first duty of the government is the security of the people and as the police and security services have said on many occasions we face a serious threat to our country.

He has since sought to explain how this must be balanced with historic values of individual liberty. This lies at the core of the multifaceted task facing the Home Office, the various aspects of which are explained in the chapters that follow.

Bryan Gibson August 2007

HOME OFFICE (HO)

Home Secretary (and other Home Office ministers)
Accountable to Parliament, including via the Home Affairs Committee

Key working partners in government include	KEY RESPONSIBILITES	Modern-day concerns include
Ministry of Justice Cabinet Office Department for Children, Schools and Families Department for Communities and Local Government Foreign Office	Safety and security	Law and order
	Protecting the public	Terrorism
	Border controls	Organized crime
	Crime prevention	Drugs, Guns, Knives
	Crime reduction	Violence, and sex crimes
Frontline services via Local police forces Non-geographic forces Serious and Organized Crime Agency (SOCA) Child Exploitation and Online Protection(CEOP) MI5 GCHQ Europol and Interpol Border staff at sea ports and airports	Safeguarding personal identity	Child protection
		Identity cards
	Shared involvement in criminal policy	Watchlists
	Animal welfare	Surveillance
	Research and statistics	Immigration
	Scientific and technological development and databases	Asylum
Many Home Office aims are also discharged via the voluntary sector, private sector and community links		Deportation
		Extradition
	Intelligence and security networks	Britishness

The Home Office and its Main Components

Contacting the Home Office

Direct Communications Unit
Home Office
2 Marsham Street
London SW1P 4DF
United Kingdom

Telephone: +44 (0) 20 7035 4848 (09.00-17.00 Monday to Friday)
Fax: +44 (0) 207 7035 4745

Minicom +44 (0) 20 7035 4742 (09.00-017.00 Monday to Friday)
(for members of the public with impaired hearing)

Web-site: www.homeoffice.gov.uk

General enquiries email: public.enquiries@homeoffice.gsi.gov.uk

The Home Office:
An Overview

CHAPTER 1

The Home Office: An Overview

The Home Office was formed as a department of government in 1782 when the existing, all-embracing office of Secretary of State was divided up between a new Home Department and a Department for Foreign Affairs. Some Home Office functions, principally national security and border controls, extend to the United Kingdom as a whole, but its jurisdiction is for the most part limited to England and Wales and there are separate arrangements in Scotland and Northern Ireland. Alongside the Treasury, these two departments have always ranked as the foremost departments of state. Thus, also, political responsibility for the Home Office, which rests with the home secretary, automatically made him[1] one of the most senior and powerful members of the Cabinet.

THE 'OLD' HOME OFFICE

It would be impossible to chart all the formative developments that have occurred and which have affected the Home Office during its three centuries and more lifespan. But it is possible to try and convey some sense of the kind and weight of its responsibilities and of how it became the organization that it had become by the early part of 2007. Essentially, as the government department responsible for internal affairs in England and Wales (what some foreign jurisdictions describe as a Ministry of the Interior) it was responsible for what can be broadly described as law and order, or keeping order, including by trying to make sure not only that crime was prevented or the offenders apprehended but also that undesirable aliens were kept out of the country or deported. Indeed, in early times, it was often concerned with putting down riots, insurrection and other major disturbances, including by calling on the militia in the days before formal police forces as well as rooting out foreign subversives in particular.[2]

Principles of justice and a network of relationships

The Home Office was always concerned with principles of justice and attempts to humanise the criminal law and its application, and its work became progressively more complex and sophisticated throughout the 19th and 20th centuries. Some former Home Office functions such as health, education and

---

[1]   Historically all home secretaries were men: see the list at the end of *Chapter 9*.

[2]   Any survey of the first decade or so of the 20th century will reveal a fear of 'strangers' akin to that of the early 2000s; and the same can be said for various other time frames.

labour (or nowadays 'employment') were transferred early on to separate and usually new ministries, and by the end of the latter century the remaining 'core tasks' involved a complicated set of relations with other government departments, especially the Lord Chancellor's Department (LCD),[3] the courts and the judiciary, and agencies such as the police, the Crown Prosecution Service (CPS) (from 1986), the originally locally-based Probation Service, and within the Home Office itself the Prison Service and the Immigration Service.

Building a safe, just and tolerant society

The main responsibilities of the old Home Office, directly or indirectly, lay across a broad spectrum spanning such areas as criminal law, policing, prisons, probation, immigration, asylum, deportation and extradition. It issued passports. Among other things and from time-to-time it took lead responsibility for such diverse matters as social equality, diversity and race relations. Eventually it came to work with individuals and communities with the aim of 'building a safe, just and tolerant society'.[4] By then, in the 21st century, its web-site also signalled that it was concerned with 'enhancing opportunities for all' in relation to which 'rights and responsibilities go hand-in-hand'.[5] Other telling slogans indicated that its remit included making sure that 'the protection and security of the public are maintained and enhanced'. This is not to say that the new Home Office described in this book has abandoned such ideas, but its livery, emphasis and presentation have altered – and some responsibilities have changed hands as will be described below and in subsequent chapters.

Departments, directorates, units and groups

The old Home Office was organized under a permanent secretary of state, on the basis of a number of departments including, notably the Criminal Department, Immigration Department, Police Department, Prison Department (after the separate Prison Commission was dissolved in 1963) and the General Department, or units such as the Research Unit (see, now *Chapter 8*) and a short-lived Probation Unit. Some of its responsibilities, chiefly those in relation to criminal justice policy, prisons and the probation service it began to style the 'Criminal Justice System' (CJS), albeit that a good part of the CJS fell outside of the remit of the Home Office, notably the courts and associated legal services. The old Home Office structure also included, e.g. its own Legal Advisors' Branch; separate and independent inspectorates of constabulary, prisons and probation; and a Prisons

---

[3] Later the Department of Constitutional Affairs (DCA) and then the Ministry of Justice (MOJ) as explained later in the chapter.

[4] A slogan that accompanied the Home Office logo.

[5] www.homeoffice.gov.uk

and Probation Ombudsman. Before May 2007, the Home Office listed several hundred sponsored or linked organizations at its web-site.

The Home Office pre-fix

Again across the years, the words 'Home Office' had become a pre-fix for various functions, tasks, regulations or instructions which are also indicative of the sprawling nature of its responsibilities, interests and influence over time. Examples of this include such diverse point of reference as:

- the Home Office Circular (or HOC), a document created centrally for distribution to stakeholders concerning, e.g. the implementation – or frequently the suggested interpretation of - legislation, including the courts[6] and other agencies involved in the criminal justice process such as the police and probation services;[7]
- the Home Office pathologist who may still attend a murder or similar crime scene or emergency and who may later give evidence in court; and
- Home Office advisor, a description given to any number of individuals from within or outside of government or, e.g. academia on whom the department might call upon from time-to-time for information, advice and expertise in a range of specialist fields.[8]

A transfer out of responsibilities

Gradually, however, the process of 'transferring out' continued. The LCD became responsible for the administration of magistrates' courts and later for human rights and elections;[9] whilst the Department for Culture, Media and Sport took over broadcasting and gambling and the Department for Communities and Local Government (as it now is) that for the Fire and Rescue Service and later community relations. Others, such as animal welfare and disaster management (formerly known as 'Civil Emergencies' or 'Civil Contingencies') remained with the Home Office or came to be shared with other government departments.

A main task was the development and implementation of new criminal justice legislation, including the creation, updating and abolition of offences, bail related procedures and the legal framework within which sentences could be

---

[6] Maybe surprisingly with hindsight, given 'judicial independence'. Rightly or wrongly, this potentially influential Home Office 'advice' could sometimes be misread by judges, etc. as 'telling' them what the law meant, or what outcomes were deemed acceptable.

[7] HOCs or their modern-day equivalent can nowadays be viewed online at www.circulars.homeoffice.gov.uk

[8] So too, e.g., historically and ominously, the Home Office List of approved public executioners in the days before the abolition of capital punishment (1965 onward); and the Home Office 'Table of Drops' setting out the length of rope that should be used.

[9] All three of which moved to the old LCD in 2001.

passed by the courts. Thus, in summary, and prior to the 2007 Home Office split there was patchwork of sometimes tenuously related responsibilities, some of which were discharged via sponsored organizations, executive agencies, directorates, or ultimately the private sector or voluntary sector, including:

- criminal law (offences and penalties); bail, procedure and sentencing (above) (now principally an MOJ task but with other departments proposing new offences in their own areas of responsibility such as the Department for Transport in relation to road traffic law or, in the case of the Home Office, public safety and public protection issues of the kind noted in *Chapter 2* or so as to ensure a ready response to terrorism as noted in *Chapter 5*);[10]
- crime reduction programmes (*Chapter 4*);
- advice and support on crime prevention (*Chapter 4*);
- co-ordination within the criminal justice system (now largely a matter for the cross-departmental Office for Criminal Justice Reform (OCJR): see under the heading *Partnership*, below);
- anti-social behaviour (see *Chapter 4*);
- mentally disordered offenders (now MOJ);
- support for victims of crime and witnesses (including via the independent Victim Support and the Witness Service) (now MOJ);
- criminal injuries compensation (now MOJ);
- community issues including volunteering (now MOJ);
- animal procedures, e.g. approving experiments or licensing laboratories;[11]
- coroners (now MOJ);
- misuse of drugs (*Chapter 8*);
- issues concerning terrorism and terrorists (*Chapter 5*);
- immigration, asylum, deportation and citizenship (*Chapter 6*); and
- general oversight of the police (*Chapter 3*), HM Prison Service (HMPS) (now MOJ) and youth justice (now a mutual interest and shared responsibility of the MOJ and a new Department for Children, Schools and Families) and the Youth Justice Board (YJB)(now MOJ).

---

[10] The Home Office used to have oversight of the criminal law, in the sense that any proposal to create a new offence needed Home Office approval and the Home Office would apply tests such as how it would be enforced; whether it was 'reasonable', e.g. what were the ingredients of the offence and what special defences were to be provided if any; whether the problem could be dealt with in other ways; whether the offence should be tried summarily by magistrates or on indictment in the Crown Court; and whether the proposed penalties were proportionate. The Cabinet's Legislation Committee wanted to be satisfied that the Home Office was happy with all that before it allowed the sponsoring department to introduce a Bill in Parliament.

[11] Attracting activists or 'terrorists' in modern times: see, generally, *Chapter 5*.

In 2002 the National Probation Service (NPS) became a directorate of the Home Office and in 2003 the National Offender Management Service (NOMS) was formed as an umbrella organization for both HMPS and the NPS under the UK's first commissioner of correctional services.[12] This is now an omnibus MOJ function. Another re-arrangement occurred in 1995 when a former responsibility of the home secretary for looking into miscarriages of justice passed from the Home Office to the Criminal Cases Review Commission (later 'Authority': CCRA) following the report of a Royal Commission on Criminal Justice that also contained certain pointers in the direction of an MOJ.[13]

The move towards a Ministry of Justice
To the tutored constitutional eye, various of the responsibilities formerly falling to the Home Office lay uneasily with what can be described as an essentially law enforcement-oriented agency. This is well-documented by David Faulkner, a former deputy secretary at the home office and now with the Oxford University Centre for Criminological Research in his authoritative work *Crime, State and Citizen: A Field Full of Folk*. After reviewing the relevant literature, he concludes that 'the case for a Department of Justice now deserves serious debate'.[14]

Such views perhaps became yet more obvious and respectable[15] in the post-Human Rights Act 1998 era when even the ancient role of the Lord Chancellor had to be revised to ensure that the UK was compliant with the fair trials principles of the European Convention On Human Rights.[16] Nonetheless, in 2003, it was still possible for home secretary David Blunkett to successfully resist a move to create an MOJ that involved some reduction in Home Office areas of responsibility together with the creation of an arguably more 'justice-friendly' split of responsibilities. But by 2007, other considerations prevailed

Famously and as already noted in the *Preface* to this work, the creation of the MOJ and, centrally, the giving up to the MOJ by the Home Office of the latter's responsibilities with regard to NOMS and the Parole Board occurred after the then home secretary, Dr John Reid, concluded that the Home Office had become 'not fit for purpose'.[17] The revelation came in the wake of events that included:

---

[12] Martin Narey. 'Corrections' is frequently used nowadays to signify penal sanctions. The term originated in the USA as a term for punishment related functions: which were, presumably, intended to correct the behaviour of offenders. It appears to have gradually entered the penal lexicon of the UK from the mid-1990s onwards.

[13] Royal Commission on Criminal Justice (1993), *Report* (Cm. 2263), HMSO.

[14] Second edition, 2006; Waterside Press. See, in particular, *Chapter 21* of that work.

[15] It is interesting that historically they may have been seen as radical or even subversive.

[16] See the companion volume to this work, *The New Ministry of Justice: An Introduction*.

[17] Government later sought to limit this to the Immigration Department. But it was widely taken to refer to the Home Office as a whole: *Chapter 10*.

- a long history of 'failure' to control actual or supposed abuses of immigration and asylum, going back to the early 1960s at least, and made worse by the convulsions that followed the collapse of communism and the opening up of the European Union to once Eastern bloc countries (*Chapter 6*);
- the London bombings of 7 July 2005 (and similar but unsuccessful attempts including that of 21 July 2005) (*Chapter 5*);[18]
- detention without trial being held to be unlawful by the courts (*Chapter 5*);
- control orders being diluted in a similar way (*Chapter 5*);
- the 'foreign prisoner crisis' whereby foreign prisoners were not being adequately considered for deportation after serving their sentences in the UK, in accordance with prior judicial recommendations (*Chapter 5*); and
- re-offending by some serious offenders after they were released from prison (see further for this and associated triggers for change in *Chapter 10*).

This list is not exhaustive. Any explanation of why events rapidly changed must have a longer and more complex background, some of which is noted in *Chapter 10* which looks at the transition into a fresh era. But, seemingly, a kind of malaise, and kind of defensiveness concerning any kind of criticism had set in on the part of ministers, perhaps exacerbated by the need to repel sometimes unjustified media criticism. Rightly or wrongly, there also seems to have been a Home Office perception that judges were becoming intransigent if they ruled against ministers on a technicality or due to international obligations under human rights law. Not only were judges openly criticised but at times lawyers were singled out as villains and 'bad mouthed' for taking technical points.[19]

THE NEW HOME OFFICE

As intimated in the *Preface*, the 'new' Home Office is represented in an amalgam of four key strands of development in United Kingdom public affairs that crystallised in 2007 and that can be usefully repeated here:

- first, the reorganization - or the 'transferring out' – that occurred at the 'old Home Office' in May of that year when some of its previously central responsibilities for the criminal law and for prisons and probation were

---

[18] All after 11 September 2001 and the destruction of the Twin Towers, New York, USA.

[19] There was even an on the hoof suggestion at one stage that the law should be altered to counter technical defences, in so much as juries would no longer be obliged to acquit an accused person in such circumstances. How this might work was not explained. More considered Home Office documents talked 'firm' rather than 'tough' about 'rebalancing the system' or 'rebalancing justice', terms that had earlier featured in the White Paper, *Justice For All* (2002; Cm.5563) that preceded the Criminal Justice Act 2003.

relinquished to a freshly created Ministry of Justice (MOJ), following earlier transfers out of the kind that have already been described;

- second, the leaner, 'slimmed down' variety of Home Office that resulted, free to concentrate on such matters as homeland security, border controls and issues of a public safety/cum/law and order nature;
- third, the advantages – but also the associated issues of accountability and legitimacy - that for the Home Office and its many partners flow from an acceleration in scientific advances - such as those in relation to cyber-technology, forensics (especially DNA), data storage and data sharing, surveillance, monitoring, intelligence gathering, risk analysis and assessment and other modern-day tools of the kind described in *Chapter 3*;
- fourth, the new and seemingly more balanced approach to the great debate on crime and punishment – and with regard to terrorism in particular – that has been accompanied latterly by a distinctly changed approach to public pronouncements, following a change of prime minister and the appointment of the UK's first woman home secretary, Jacqui Smith.[20]

As also noted in the *Preface* other analyses are quite possible and some commentators might point, in particular, to the unprecedented build up in criminal justice legislation and maybe prison overcrowding. As explained in *Chapter 10*, an estimated 3,000 new offences were created in the decade to 2007 whilst the prison population had risen from around 60,000 to some 80,000; and from 42,000 to 60,000 in the decade before that. Whatever the justification this all led to noticeable tensions including from time-to-time as between the Government, the police, the courts, the correctional services and civil liberties and penal reform groups; the best recipe for progress. Signs of change were soon evident following the 'Home Office split' as noted at various points in this book.

Key objectives of the new Home Office
According to its own post-Home Office split web-site,[21] the Home Office, in its new guise, is the government department responsible for leading

> the national effort to protect the public from terrorism, crime and anti-social behaviour: we secure our borders and welcome legal migrants and visitors. We safeguard identity and citizenship. We help build the security, justice and respect that enable people to prosper in a free and tolerant society.

As noted in *Chapter 4*, targeting 'respect' has moved from the margins of official thinking on crime prevention and crime reduction to its present mainstream role

---

[20] For a useful profile see that in the *Sunday Times*, 22 July 2007.
[21] www.homeoffice.gov.uk

in the relatively short time since the first UK anti-social behaviour orders (ASBOs) were introduced by the Crime and Disorder Act 1998.

The work of the Home Office is organized around what its web-site describes as seven key objectives contributing 'to [its] overriding mission to protect the public' as it seeks to turn this into a reality. These are 'to:

- help people feel safer in their homes and local communities;
- support visible, responsive and accountable policing;
- protect the public from terrorist attack;
- cut crime, especially violent, drug and alcohol-related crime;
- strengthen our borders, fast track asylum decisions, ensure and enforce compliance with our immigration laws, and boost Britain's economy;
- safeguard people's identity and the privileges of citizenship; and
- work with our partners to build an efficient, effective and proportionate Criminal Justice System (CJS)'.

Each of these objectives consists of a huge agenda in itself as described in the chapters that follow. The last item, partnership, deserves special mention here and demonstrates that the Home Office remains involved in and committed to other shared objectives within what can be described as a new structure for the CJS and beyond. This is explored further later in this chapter.

The basic Home Office remit
Its remit, directly or indirectly and either in its own right or in partnership (below), and in terms of the discharge of its responsibilities on an everyday basis, can now, post-MOJ (below), be summarised as:

- public safety and the protection of the public (*Chapter 2*);
- the police and policing via independent local police forces and local police authorities (*Chapter 3*);
- crime prevention and crime reduction as the lead department but in partnership with other government departments (*Chapter 4*);
- terrorism and other emergencies, including through an Office for Security and Counter-Terrorism that provides advice to ministers, develops policy and provides security measures (*Chapter 5*);
- border controls, asylum and immigration via a unified Border Agency or as it has been more dramatically described a 'Border Force' (*Chapter 6*);
- safeguarding personal identity, e.g. through the development of identity cards and associated developments (*Chapter 7*); and

- a range of miscellaneous responsibilities linked to the above such as the pursuit of scientific development and research (*Chapter 8*).[22]

It was reported by the national media that as part of the Home Office split John Reid, the then home secretary, sought unsuccessfully to wrest MI6 from the Foreign and Commonwealth Office, it having been argued for some time in certain quarters that the security services might be better under one roof, or possibly combined. The Home Office retains its pre-existing links with MI5 and in common with the Foreign Office, the government listening station GCHQ, all with strong links to the Cabinet Office as described in *Chapter 5*.

RELATIONSHIP TO THE NEW MINISTRY OF JUSTICE

The relationship between the 'old' Home Office and the 'old' LCD was at one time rather distant, reflecting the Home Office's own concern not to appear to be interfering with the judiciary, with which the LCD was closely identified due to the fact that the majority of judges and magistrates were appointed by the Lord Chancellor and that as head of the judiciary he[23] could sit as a judge (and some Lord Chancellors regularly did so).[24] Various protocols and understandings, unwritten but absorbed by civil servants and practitioners within the culture of their own departments or fields of work, existed to protect both the Home Office and LCD/DCA from judicial interference, and similarly the judiciary itself from interference by the HO or LCD/DCA or any other executive department. The relationship became closer with attempts to 'manage' the Criminal Justice System (CJS) that began during the 1980s and under the more stringent financial regime which the Treasury was imposing at that time. The situation needed careful handling at a time when the Home Office was beginning to include legislation on sentencing in its attempts to manage the system in pursuit of the Government's insistence on 'efficiency, economy and effectiveness'.

There was also, with hindsight, the somewhat peculiar scenario that emerged in the 1980s and early-1990s whereby practitioners and the courts began to strongly influence the shape of criminal justice policy by taking what were commonly described as 'initiatives', according to their own perceptions of what

---

[22] See also *Chapter 8* and *Appendix II* to this work.
[23] All Lord Chancellors have been men.
[24] Notably, Lord Hailsham in the 1970s. Under the Constitutional Reform Act 2005 these and other judicial functions of the Lord Chancellor were switched to the Lord Chief Justice. But the former has a statutory duty to protect the independence of the judiciary, as stressed by the first new-style Secretary of State for Justice and Lord Chancellor, Jack Straw in 2007 on his first day in office.

sentencing was intended to achieve. Central amongst these was what became the alternative to custody movement from the mid-1980s onwards. Among connected phenomena was a fall in the numbers of juveniles being sent to custody from a high of around 8,000 a year to some 2,000. This and similar initiatives that served to hold the adult prison population at around 45,000 as opposed to the 80,000 population of today were largely determined 'on the ground', sometimes via multi-agency strategies, but few of which central government felt able directly to support except by general statements that may have appeared in White Papers, Green Papers and legislation for the courts to use. It was largely, perhaps, this lack of coordination as between government policy and often local and variable decision-making[25] that led to moves to create the statutory sentencing framework that appeared first in the Criminal Justice Act 1991 and later that of 2003.

Encouraging coherence and consistency

Much may have been achieved by the above in terms of progressive thinking about sentencing, but it is also possible to describe that scenario as what, in purely political or managerial terms, might nowadays be viewed as wholly dysfunctional. The tension arose because, historically speaking, there never was any such thing as a fixed sentencing rule or framework for decision-making. Indeed, the further back one looks, statements, e.g. about the purposes of sentencing were passed from judge to judge, magistrate to magistrate or judge to magistrate via the appeals process or 'training days'. What a Crown Court judge said at a meeting of magistrates, e.g. about the need to lock up a particular kind of offender (or not as the case may be) could set the pattern and become a point of reference for years to come. The conventional wisdom and oddments of law about sentencing were in the 1970s distilled in a Home Office publication, *The Sentence of the Court*,[26] a fact that now seems surprising in an era when the responsibility for such legislation has been passed to the MOJ and, through it, as to advice on sentencing, the MOJ-sponsored SGC. *The Sentence of the Court* shows that great emphasis was placed by courts on such 'general [but then largely unqualified and sometimes uncertain] objects of sentencing' as punishment, reparation, retribution, deterrence, reflecting public concern and rehabilitation. Additionally, great weight was given to a relatively small number of key rulings

---

[25] Sometimes dubbed 'justice by geography'.

[26] The first Home Office edition was published in 1980. Four later editions were published by Waterside Press (1995, 1998, 2000, 2002) after the Home Office and LCD signalled that they had no further interest in that publication. This is interesting in the context of the present discussion, in that these were created by a group of interested practitioners who, in effect (and in conjunction with the Judicial Studies Board (JSB)) determined the content of what became widely used, quasi-official texts and guidance.

of the Court of Appeal with regard to appeals against sentences imposed by the Crown Court and leading commentators, foremost amongst whom was the highly respected Cambridge University-based academic Dr David Thomas QC.

Moves towards a more structured approach to sentencing

As already indicated, this may have worked in a functional sense and during an era when legislation itself was largely unconcerned with anything more than handing to the courts a range of powers, but it hardly stood scrutiny in terms of a coherent approach to the issue of sentencing a whole, its costs, resource demands and overall purposes. Commentators such as David Thomas were saying things to the effect, 'Leave it to the judges'. Whilst such sentiments corresponded with a meticulously constitutional approach to judicial independence, they perhaps left too much to chance; and within the Home Office itself attempts were being made to make sentencing more coherent within a joined up system of working in which the effect of decision-making took greater account of penal strategy across the board.[27] Against this background, the creation of a new-style MOJ capable of co-ordinating criminal policy, resources (including those of HM Prison Service (HMPS) and the National Probation Service (NPS)), research, statistics and input by the Lord Chancellor to an independent SGC can be argued as a major advance and long overdue.[28] If tensions have existed in recent years with the judiciary, they have tended to be in areas where judicial discretion has been constrained, as with mandatory or minimum sentences for certain serious or repeated offences. In the end result, the relevant doctrine is that of the supremacy of Parliament via which and subject to any wider human rights considerations, such decisions are made via the democratic process.[29]

Shifts in responsibility – the new MOJ

Since the Home Office split of 2007 and accompanying transfer of responsibilities to the MOJ, the latter's duties and responsibilities can be summarised as follows:[30]

---

[27] Key events of this era included the Criminal Justice Acts of 1982, 1987 and 1991 and a Parole Review of 1988. *The Parole System in England and Wales: Report of the Review Committee* (Chair Lord Carlisle), Cm. 532, HMSO. See, further, *The New Ministry of Justice*. A powerful critic of 'leaving it to the judges' was Professor (then Dr) Andrew Ashworth who was one of the first commentators to propose a sentencing council.

[28] For some further comments on sentencing see the end of *Chapter 2*; and for an excellent survey of events relating to this period, see *Crime, State and Citizen: A Field Full of Folk* (Second edition 2006), Faulkner D, Waterside Press.

[29] This may beg the question of how effective that process is in terms of real democracy, but that is a different issue, and one now being pursued in the Government/MOJ White Paper, *The Governance of Britain* (2007; Cm 7170).

[30] A full list of MOJ responsibilities is contained in *The Ministry of Justice, etc.* (above): see, in particular, *Chapter 1* and *Appendix II* of that accompanying volume.

- working 'trilaterally' with the other departments that make up the central government strands of the Criminal Justice System (CJS), i.e. the Home Office and Office of the Attorney General (see also later in this chapter under 'Partnership and Shared Responsibility');
- HM Courts Service (HMCS), that now oversees the administration of all of the civil, family and criminal courts in England and Wales;
- support for the judiciary, including:
  - appointments via the newly created Judicial Appointments Commission (JAC);
  - an Office of Judicial Complaints (OJC);
  - a Judicial Office (JO), or secretariat, to serve the Lord Chief Justice and senior judiciary; and
  - a Judicial Communications Office for communications with and between judges and also magistrates;
- the Tribunals Service across the whole of the UK;
- the National Offender Management Service (NOMS), responsible for the commissioning of correctional services and their administration throughM Prison Service (HMPS), the National Probation Service (NPS) (both services were formerly major Home Office responsibilities) and in future from competing independent providers of services and facilities;
- sponsorship of:
  - HM Inspectorates of Prison and Probation (formerly Home Office);
  - Independent Monitoring Boards (IMBs) (formerly Home Office);[31]
  - the Parole Board (formerly Home Office);
  - the Prisons and Probation Ombudsman (formerly Home Office);
- legal aid and the more wide-ranging Community Legal Service (CLS), through the Legal Services Commission (LSC);
- sentencing policy, including sponsorship of:
  - the Sentencing Guidelines Council (SGC); and
  - Sentencing Advisory Panel (SAP) (both formerly Home Office);
- criminal, civil, family and administrative law (the first of these formerly Home Office);
- sponsorship of the Law Commission (always an LCD/DCA function);
- hosting the Office for Criminal Justice Reform (OCJR);
- the Privy Council Secretariat and the Office of the Judicial Committee of the Privy Council; and
- constitutional affairs, including:

---

[31] Formerly Boards of Visitors, i.e. visitors to prisons with authority to enter their allocated prison establishment at any time and with access to prisoners, charged with reporting to (in future) the Secretary of State for Justice/Lord Chancellor annually and in relation to individual incidents that may occur, at IMB members' discretion.

—House of Lords reform;
—electoral reform and democratic engagement;
—civil and human rights;
—freedom of information; and
—the management of UK constitutional arrangements and
 relationships including with devolved administrations for Wales,
 Scotland and Northern Ireland and Crown dependencies.

The Home Office earlier relinquished its former responsibility for investigating miscarriages of justice when this was transferred to the Criminal Cases Review Commission (CCRC), an independent public body that was set up in 1997 under the Criminal Appeal Act 1995. The first cases of widespread public concern to be dealt with by the CCRC[32] were those of the Guildford Four who were wrongly convicted of the Irish Republican Army (IRA) Guildford pub bombings of 1974, in which five people were murdered and 50 others maimed or injured.

PARTNERSHIP AND SHARED RESPONSIBILITY

Partnership is a device for cooperation between different agencies and services that grew out of initiatives to encourage multi-agency liaison and 'working together'. It is generally accepted that where partnership occurs those taking part retain there own professional boundaries, independence and roles but seek to enhance outcomes by sharing, e.g. knowledge, information or resources as appropriate. The situation is sometimes described as one of 'interdependence'.

Coordination at national level
Whilst not perhaps technically described as 'partnership' the first and highest tier of liaison, at the macro or central governmental level consists of a range of involvements including established links with:

- other government departments such as the MOJ, Office of the Attorney General and what is now, since July 2007, a Department for Children, Schools and Families, both directly and via a multi-agency Cabinet Committee on Crime and the Criminal Justice System (CCCCJS);
- the Department of Communities and Local Government concerning such matters as race, religion, social cohesion, civil renewal and regeneration;
- the police and the security services MI5 and GCHQ (*Chapters 3* and *5*);
- the Commissioner of the Metropolitan Police Service (MPS) and Association of Chief Police Officers (ACPO) (*Chapter 3*);
- the various nationally based police organizations including the National Police Improvement Agency and Serious and Organized Crime Agency

---

[32] In its then guise of the Criminal Cases Review Authority (CCRA).

(SOCA) and related intelligence, databases and facilities for pursuing the proceeds of crime by tracking-down and where possible seizing the assets of offenders and generally disrupting organized crime (*Chapters 3* and *10*);

- other nationwide agencies such as the MOJ-led Courts Service, HM Prison Service (especially vis-à-vis the release and subsequent supervision of certain offenders) and National Probation Service (NPS) who share comparable aims and objectives or encompass areas of common concern such as crime prevention, crime reduction or protecting the public;
- a range of regulatory 'watchdogs' with their own administrative powers to regulate affairs in particular areas of day-to-day life;
- organizations from the third sector[33] in so far as these operate at a national level, many of whom provide resources designed to reduce crime or assist and support ex-offenders who are going straight;
- the National Criminal Justice Board (NCJB) that discusses broadly related issues as between the heads of the various agencies;
- European and other partner governments, both directly and via organizations such as Interpol and Europol; and
- national media, including influential programmes such as *Crimewatch*.[34]

Partnership at the local level

At a micro, day-to-day, practical or 'grass roots' and more locally-based level, delivery of the services on which the Home Office necessarily relies include, e.g.:

- the Crown Prosecution Service (CPS) (whose head, the director of public prosecutions reports to the attorney general) (*Chapter 3*);
- Neighbourhood Watch and similar schemes such as Business Watch, Farm Watch and Boat Watch;
- local courts in terms of the provision of support services and general administrative matters, principally via links between police 'criminal justice offices' or joint local police/CPS Criminal Justice Units (CJUs);
- local prisons;
- local probation services;
- Local Criminal Justice Boards (LCJBs) and their participating agencies;
- local authorities, especially in terms of their own crime prevention and crime reduction initiatives;
- Crimestoppers, an independent UK-wide charity 'working to stop crime' and that now operates via the internet as well as by telephone (enabling crimes to be reported more easily) and similar organizations;

---

[33] 'Third sector' is usually taken to signify voluntary and community organizations, faith groups and what are sometimes termed 'social enterprises'. The 'private sector' is sometimes called the second sector. Many local organizations of both kinds also provide resources or services. See also generally, www.thirdsector.co.uk

[34] BBC1 TV. *Crimewatch* features unsolved crimes and invites viewers to 'telephone in'.

- the many more locally based or locally designated bodies whose aims and objectives encompass areas in common of the kind already noted above;
- local media; and
- informal networks of informants who pass information to the police.

There is also a parallel need for managerial arrangements and understandings that translate effectively across hierarchies and levels of authority; and are as comprehensible to heads of departments as they are to local managers and grass roots – e.g. the front line police officer making an arrest, the Crown prosecutor deciding whether prosecution is in the public interest, the probation officer in the community (or sometimes prison) setting out his or her recommendations in a pre-sentence report (PSR), the prison officer on the landing preparing a sentence plan – and adequate safeguards for *judicial independence permitting* – for the individual judge or magistrate sitting in court to decide upon the merits of an individual case. Such strategies must also survive over time so that they are equally relevant and workable to the Parole Board at the 'back end' of a sentence many years on and in a possibly changed sentencing milieu.

THE NEW ERA

It is easy for anyone, whatever their subject, to suggest that events are about to enter a new era and then to predict that it will come to pass. But maybe the pointers above are enough to suggest that it is at least a time to 'watch this space' as the changes described in this book take hold. At the end of the book, in *Chapter 10, Into a Fresh Era* an attempt is made to assess the depth of change that the Home Office split appears to have precipitated. It is early days, but the changes already seem to have triggered a change of tone or temperature, as indicated by (unusually) supportive media reports such as that which followed the Glasgow Airport terrorist attack of July 2007 in which following a report to Parliament the home secretary was - according to what is admittedly merely a press anecdote - 'praised by all sides for her calmness and confidence with which she had reacted to the crisis'.[35] This is just one of a number of similar indicators that may bode well for the future, further examples of which feature in the chapters and appendices that follow.

---

[35] *The Guardian,* 3 July 2007, p.6. 'Ministers step up hearts and minds campaign'.

Public Safety, Liberty and Protecting the Public

CHAPTER 2

Public Safety, Liberty and Protecting the Public

Public safety and the protection of the public lie at the heart of the functions of any government, of whatever political hue – and whether from external threats such as war, international terrorism or other forms of external aggression, or (as per virtually any society)[1] from 'home grown' threats such as violent attack, uprising, insurrection, revolution, civil war or the work of activists. Organized crime and terrorism nowadays feature prominently alongside more basic concerns about risks from individual high-risk or 'heavy end' offenders. At an every day practical level, protecting citizens so that that they can go about their daily lives without being deprived of their physical or fiscal integrity requires that safeguards are in place to protect them from a range of offenders including:

- those involved in violent gangs;
- those involved in the underworld, organized crime or 'drugs world';
- those who carry or use weapons such as guns or knives;
- those affected by anger, rage or serious forms of mental impairment;
- the occasional serial killer;[2]
- sexual predators, especially serial rapists and paedophiles;
- terrorists and people involved in other forms of extremism or direct action who may be driven by a quasi-political or religious imperative;
- fraudsters and other dishonest offenders, especially those who nowadays operate on a large scale (including remotely over the internet) or who rely on the use of intimidation, bullying, coercion or fear; and
- those who place people at risk from unsafe systems of health and safety at work or in relation to passenger travel, entertainment, sport or the like.

The need for a wide range of protections
The above snapshot emphasises the breadth of the different kinds of protection that need to be in place; none of which standing alone is likely to protect everyone from every hazard. Hence the need for specialist forms of policing as described in *Chapter 3*, a welter of crime prevention measures (*Chapter 4*) and the large scale resources deployed to combat terrorism, nowadays generally treated as a distinct, if also partially integral, form of policing (*Chapter 5*). This chapter considers a number of more general issues. It is important, e.g. to note

---

1   There are said to be remote communities where crime or internal threats do not exist.
2   For an up-to-date treatment, see *Serial Killers: Hunting Britons and their Victims* (2007), Wilson, D, Waterside Press.

at the outset that threats may not fall tidily into compartments: the violent activities of terrorists – already 'criminals' on that account[3] - may occur in tandem with other crimes to fund that terrorism, or 'terrorism' may sometimes be used by terrorists more equivocally as a cover for what is in reality violent or dishonest appropriation of property, criminal damage, arson or money laundering. There is an analogy here with those less responsible commercial concerns that flout the rules in general, not just those relating, e.g. to the health and safety of employees, but who then risk prosecution as part of an economic calculation driven by the need to make a profit (or limit losses). Hence the need for what are sometimes termed 'watchdogs', regulatory authorities with their own powers to levy administrative fines; and a range of law enforcement officers and public prosecutors going far beyond the confines of the everyday civil police and their working partner, the Crown Prosecution Service (CPS). All this is a form of public protection in the broad sense of that term and much of that work involves public safety, even if, sometimes, as with food safety, the threat is of a less immediate kind than an attack with a knife or bomb.

Countless strategies, schemes, courses and initiatives exist to protect the public from crime. They are sometimes classified as 'primary', 'secondary' and 'tertiary' prevention. Primary prevention consists of mostly physical measures to make crime harder to commit or easier to detect – improved security, CCTV, 'designing out' crime from public buildings and housing estates. Secondary prevention relates to the treatment of convicted offenders and especially to sentencing and measures such as electronic monitoring or 'tagging' (see under *Protecting the Public* below).[4] Tertiary prevention relates to longer-term measures designed to reform offenders or at least to reduce the chances that they will re-offend. Hence, e.g. various accredited courses and programmes are operated by HM Prison Service (HMPS) and the National Probation Service (NPS), including those that serve to support the work of the Parole Board (all, now, following the Home Office split, MOJ responsibilities). Such functions often rely on a wide range of partner organizations in the public sector, private sector and voluntary sector. Likewise sentencing powers themselves may be directed towards protecting the public from violent and sexual offenders, as explained under the main heading *Protecting the Public*.

---

[3] A point regularly made at Home Office web-sites and in Government pronouncements. In 2007, Tarique Gaffur, an assistant commissioner in the Metropolitan Police Service and the UK's most senior Muslim police officer, when announcing the creation of a new Safety Foundation intended to identify extremists via the cooperation of members of the Muslim community and to examine 'the dynamics of disaffection', used the words 'cabal of psychopaths' to describe would-be suicide bombers.

[4] And for a more detailed treatment, the companion work, *The New Ministry of Justice*.

It is also far more likely nowadays than ever before that sound information will exist on police files, databases and other forms of intelligence that will help to avoid people becoming victims.[5] The case of Ian Huntley is often cited as a watershed in this regard. Huntley murdered two young girls, Jessica Chapman and Holly Wells, at the school where he worked as a caretaker at Soham, Cambridgeshire. The events revealed 'serious failings' and 'potentially significant errors' in police record keeping (Huntley had been accused of having sex with underage girls and of rape several times in the past), inter-force communications (he had moved several hundred miles south) and employment vetting to work with children. Hence, also, e.g. such key developments as the Sex Offender Register, the Department for Children, Schools and Families 'List 99' (that in almost all cases excludes people who are on it from working with children) and the increasingly developed arrangements that exist to inform victims of the fact that 'their' offender is due for release from prison and of his or her whereabouts after this occurs. Similarly, a diluted form of the USA-based Megan's Law has been introduced in several pilot areas of the UK.[6] Many such developments are tentative or in their infancy in the search for 21st century solutions crime. Others, such as Multi-agency Protection Panel Arrangements (MAPPAs) are well established in most parts of the country (see later in this chapter). There have been suggestions for other watch lists, including in relation to terrorism. These already exist in relation to the specific context of air and sea travel and are being constantly enhanced in terms of their content and reach (*Chapter 5*).

Mental impairment

There is one category of 'offender' from whom the public must be protected even though this may be due to no fault on the part of the individual. Hence, those who present a risk can be detained under various provisions of mental health legislation. In the extreme, an offender guilty of a serious offence such as murder may enter a special plea of insanity as a result of which he or she will be detained for life in a special hospital as an alternative to serving a mandatory sentence of life imprisonment. More problematic are those people who are known to represent a high-risk, are clinically impaired, but for whom

---

[5]   See the *Bichard Inquiry Report* (2004) HC 653.

[6]   Sometimes called Sarah's Law after eight-year-old Sarah Payne who was taken from the roadside and killed by Roy Whiting in West Sussex in 2000. Megan's Law is a scheme whereby citizens can find out from the police whether a local sex offender lives in their area. Such schemes are contentious in that they tend to encourage vigilantes and are not infallible in terms of identifying the correct person as an offender. There is now talk of a Madeleine's Law following the disappearance of Madeleine McCann in Spain in 2007.

there is no provision or authority to hold them, something that led to a review of such powers and fresh, though still incomplete, legislation in this regard.[7]

PUBLIC SAFETY VERSUS INDIVIDUAL FREEDOM

Any move to increase public safety, in so far as it involves restrictions on the freedom of citizens in general, attracts attention from civil libertarians and human rights campaigners. This is not necessarily because they are against such measures *per se* as much as all such measures risk being abused in their application. The history of such measures and the sometimes questionable basis upon which the authorities have sought to act over the centuries is both colourful and often full of controversy.[8]

The phenomenon of protest and Government response is particularly to the fore with regard to freedom of expression and association. Naturally, in a free and democratic society people should, as a fundamental right, be able to peacefully gather to discuss their concerns and to express their views not simply via established democratic processes but through open protests, demonstrations, marches, placards, picketing, a free press and other avenues for uncensored public comment such as the theatre. These are also human rights guaranteed by Articles 9, 10 and 11 of the European Convention on Human Rights (ECHR). There is thus sometimes, in this particular context, an almost instant reaction to anything done in the name of the state that is claimed to be for the general protection of the public; when governments may also be accused of being paternalistic or of operating a 'nanny state'.[9] There is, of course, a sometimes thin line between well-meaning, innocent and legitimate protest and direct action or similarly subversive activities. Predictably, following a series of appeals in the courts, the right to protest on the streets of the UK is now emerging from an era of unduly repressive measures and arguably aggressive or at least enthusiastic, terrorism legislation-led, policing. This aspect is again mentioned in *Chapter 5* in relation to private sector attempts to establish a wide-ranging protest exclusion zone around Heathrow Airport in 2007.

Britain's radical heritage
Problems also arise because what was once perceived as a threat to national security (below) or public order may actually lead to progress in its wake. There

---

[7] Further information about this specialist area of public protection should be sought in dedicated works. Mental health is now an MOJ rather than Home Office responsibility.

[8] Some examples appear in *Chapter 8*

[9] Sometimes described as an integral part of Anglo-Saxon culture but it is clearly at least a Europe-wide phenomenon and also reflected, e.g. in the USA.

is indeed a long and proud tradition concerning what has been described as 'Britain's radical heritage'.[10] In modern times, concerns about manipulation of the democratic process have been exacerbated by revelations under the Freedom of Information Act 2000 of the activities of MI5 and Special Branch (*Chapter 5*) in relation to such matters as the Campaign for Nuclear Disarmament (CND), the miners' strike of 1984 and generally in relation to communism ever since the Second World War, including in terms of undercover infiltration. Such revelations occurred at a time when there has been growing concern in some quarters about the taking of increasingly broad powers in the name of terrorism; followed in some instances by their application to non-terrorist situations.[11]

Sometimes, notions of public protection are inextricably intertwined with theories[12] of oppression, repression, censorship (sometimes called 'gagging') and the idea of a police state (see the specific mention of this *Chapter 3*). Such debates are to be found not simply at a political or operational level but at philosophical, criminological, ideological or jurisprudential ones. In practical terms, the Home Office has often featured at the centre of such debates as the government department faced with ensuring law and order. During the decade when prime minister Tony Blair was in office after the New Labour Government came to power in the UK in 1997 there appears to have been decreasing regard for the finer points of such arguments or the lessons of history. Whether this will change in what would appear to be a new era of democratic engagement, if that is now what exists in the UK (*Chapter 10*), remains to be seen.

A question of balance

The issue of 'freedom under the law' is not of course confined to freedom of expression and neither is it limited by time or the individuals who are in power. The broader context is well summarised in the words of David Faulkner, a former deputy secretary of state at the Home Office and now an expert in constitutional matters at the Oxford Centre for Criminological Research in a pamphlet written in 1991:

> Just as the secretary of state was a powerful and sometimes suspicious figure in Tudor England, so the Home Office is a powerful department in modern Britain ... [All of its] functions involve balance between the protection of the public and the wider interests of society on the one hand, and the liberty of the subject on the other –

---

[10] Readers wishing to pursue this are referred to a series of articles published in the *Guardian* newspaper during 2006/7 under that title.

[11] Such as the Camp for Climate Change near Heathrow Airport in 2007. In one month after attempted car-bombings in London in 2007 there were 11,000 uses of terrorist powers to search people in the streets as against five such searches in Scotland during the same time frame (BBC Radio Five Live news item said to be based on police figures).

[12] Or sometimes, perhaps, conspiracy theories.

the principle of 'freedom under the law'. That balance is at the heart of the department's business, it depends partly on the vision and integrity of the department's own staff, and partly on the law and administrative procedures within which we operate. These procedures are rightly subject to constant questioning and sometimes revision.[13]

Considerations of what is nowadays described as 'proportionality' should be to the fore of all aspects of Government and understood by ministers, officials and practitioners alike from a range of disciplines.

PROTECTING THE PUBLIC AND SENTENCING

Under the Criminal Justice Act 1991, the 'protection of the public' became one of the bases on which people can be sent to custody and for determining the length or amount of an offender's sentence. It remains a general statutory objective after being included in the first statutory purposes of sentencing as set out in the Criminal Justice Act 2003;[14] and also under that same Act in relation to the protection of the public from certain dangerous and high-risk offenders.[15] It is thus a key aim both of policing (*Chapter 3*) and sentencing (see later in this chapter). Hence, the existence of various specialist police or other law enforcement units whose purpose it is to target people who place the general public at-risk of harm, especially serious harm, and the creation of related databases and lists by the police or other agencies.

Sentencing generally
The sentencing of offenders is not a function of the Home Office, rather of the courts, whose administration falls squarely within the remit of the Ministry of Justice (MOJ). There are a number of ways in which that department can seek to influence the broad levels of sentences, say for violent or sexual offences, offences of dishonesty or those involving drugs or alcohol. Principally nowadays, this is via the Sentencing Guidelines Council (SGC) in relation to which the Secretary of State for Justice and Lord Chancellor has certain duties and responsibilities in place of the home secretary who discharged these pre-May 2007 and the creation of the MOJ. The Lord Chief Justice heads the SGC, which for the largest part is made up of members of the judiciary, mainly judges of various levels within the judicial hierarchy but also magistrates (also known as justices of the peace). It is the judiciary that – under a constitutional principle

[13] Taken from an unpublished internal Home Office 'Occasional Paper in Administrative Studies', No. 2 of 1991. Available on www.watersidepress.co.uk
[14] See section 142 of the 2003 Act.
[15] See, in particular, Part 12, Chapter 5 of the 2003 Act: sections 224-236.

designed to ensure and safeguard the separation of executive, legislative and judicial powers – decides what sentence will be passed on an offender in a given case. Over and above any guidelines issued by the SGC, judges and magistrates must, of course, have regard to any statutory purposes of sentencing of the kind noted above. As has been explained, these include the protection of the public. More generally, the MOJ includes public protection within its more broadly stated aims, as do other departments working in partnership with the Home Office. There is thus a delicate and sensitive balance in this regard that must be maintained by any home secretary as further commented upon in *Chapters 9* and *10*.[16] It will suffice here to note that they have, alongside other provisions concerning life sentences and tariff setting by the courts – been criticised as an interference with judicial discretion – or at least constraining judges from doing justice on the multifarious facts of individual cases – especially in relation to the substantial indeterminate sentences for public protection (SPPs)[17] that have been passed since the 2003 Act came into force, some 4,000 in total, serving to fuel an unprecedented expansion in the prisoner population. It is not that judges are against public protection, which would be a ludicrous proposition, but that, in a nutshell, many consider that they are being required by law to pass disproportionately long sentences accompanied by extensive post-custody supervision in even the least serious of such cases.[18]

PROTECTING THE PUBLIC AND CRIME PREVENTION

Many devices, arrangements and responses to crime exist to protect the public and that the Home Office may seek to influence – and without which it cannot begin to achieve some of its key aims - but that are beyond its immediate control.

Violent and other high-risk offenders

As already indicated, special sentencing provisions exist for the purposes of protecting the public from a range of violent offenders, sexual offenders and other people who present a high risk to the public if they are at-large or unsupervised; and as to terrorism, it has been suggested on various occasions that the UK might enter a derogation concerning detention without trial and/or control orders with regard to suspected terrorists (*Chapter 5*) but the overall

---

[16] The sentence-related aspects of protecting the public are further touched on in the companion to this work, *The New Ministry of Justice,* and in further detail in *Introduction to the Criminal Justice Act 2003: A Guide to the New Procedures and Sentencing* (2004), Gibson B, Waterside Press.

[17] Sometimes called IPPs, i.e. 'imprisonment for public protection', or even ISPPs.

[18] Further aspects of sentencing are noted in *The New Ministry of Justice.*

political momentum seems to have been against such a course. Much work to protect citizens by preventing and reducing crime (*Chapter 4*) in relation to these high-risk or 'heavy end' offenders occurs through the use of risk assessments.

Risk assessment and risk levels

Risk assessment (sometimes called 'risk prediction') is a term that is nowadays. applied across a whole range of situations in which a critical decision has to be made, the results of which could affect public safety or security, e.g. in relation to the policing of an event, diplomatic or witness protection, a raid of premises, hostage-taking, interception of a criminal gang or air and sea travel in particular. Sometimes what are called 'risk levels' are applied according to set criteria. Similar principles govern authorisation of the use of firearms, Taser-guns (sometimes called 'stun guns') or CS gas by a police officer or a member of the security services, albeit that some decisions need to be made at the officer's discretion, instantaneously. Proportionality is a key factor in all such situations.

Risk and offenders In the context of an individual offender or suspect, 'risk assessment' (which in the context of sentencing is now an MOJ responsibility) signifies a professional evaluation as to whether or not he or she might commit an offence. It is thus an aid to decision-making, in practice connoting the relative likelihood of his or her offending or re-offending. Various tools exist to support such decisions, including the Offender Analysis and Assessment System (OASYS) employed by the National Probation Service (NPS) or HM Prison Service (HMPS). Comparable assessments are also made by doctors in the case of people who are mentally impaired.[19] It is sometimes said that the Criminal Justice System (CJS) is risk averse in the sense that practitioners are nowadays reluctant to take risks with offenders in a way in which they may have been prepared to do in the past, partly driven by the public outcry that has followed a limited number of high profile risk assessment failures. The Home Office is not now, post-Home Office split, to the fore of such matters, but often, until now, it has been the target of criticism for independent decisions of, say, the Parole Board; often seeking to initiate or conduct a review.[20] Since the responsibility for

---

[19] Or to use the politically correct terminology, people who are 'mentally challenged'.

[20] Hence, notoriously, before the Home Office relinquished responsibility with regard to the Parole Board a number of high profile cases in which ex-prisoners had gone on commit murder or other serious offences. Notoriously, these include the case of Anthony Rice a sex offender who murdered a woman whilst on parole in Winchester in 2005. Andrew Bridges, HM Chief Inspector of Probation, attracted a brief public outcry after saying that the number of such released prisoners re-offending was 'tiny' in comparison to the number of parole decisions; around 100 prisoners had committed 'serious' crimes while on licence out of the 20,000 offenders under supervision.

such matters was passed to the MOJ, the Home Office must now rely on close cooperation between that department and the front line agencies with which it is closely concerned in order to protect the public, especially links to the police.

Within the prisons and according to the particular regime there are a now range of accredited sex offender treatment programmes (SOTPs) that must be completed by certain offenders before they can be considered for parole; whilst other programmes focus on anger, rage and the use of drugs or alcohol. Another response to risk is the creation of watch lists of the kind noted in other chapters.

Multi-agency Protection Panel Arrangements (MAPPAs)
MAPPAs were introduced by the Criminal Justice and Courts Services Act 2000 that drew on the earlier work of police and the then local probation services. In effect, the 2000 Act required the police and the modern-day NPS to work together so as to manage the risks posed by violent offenders and sexual offenders in the community. MAPPAs were further strengthened following the Criminal Justice Act 2003 which placed an obligation on the police and NPS to work with alongside other key agencies, including housing departments, social services and health services in each local area. MAPPAs monitor and manage dangerous and high-risk offenders.[21] Lay members from local communities are also invited to join professional staff on strategy boards that oversee the work of MAPPAs. There is a database of violent and sexual offenders (known as VISOR). Offenders are likely, in the first instance, to come onto a local scheme on release from prison or from special hospital under a life licence, parole conditions or supervision under mental health legislation.

NATIONAL SECURITY

The security of the state as opposed to that of individual citizens, groups or communities is frequently referred to as 'state security' or, more commonly, perhaps, 'national security'. National security may sometimes need to take precedence over personal or private rights, including human rights – whether under the inherent emergency powers of the home secretary or other ministers or emergency legislation (*Chapter 5*). In this, the Home Office is heavily reliant on the work, intelligence and information of the police (*Chapter 3*) and security services (*Chapter 5*). Conversely, certain actions or events may render someone free from prosecution, conviction and sentence if carried out in the broader national interest, as where force is used to prevent some imminent and serious attack. Other such defences may be provided by statute (as in the Protection from

---

[21] High risk offenders are sometimes referred to as 'high profile offenders': not to be confused with those offenders whose crimes become headline news.

Harassment Act 1997 that allows people to be inconvenienced without redress on this ground), at common law (as with reasonable self-defence or similarly proportionate acts for the protection of property). A Crown prosecutor may discontinue a prosecution under the public interest test or the attorney general may intervene to stop a prosecution.[22] Related areas of the law concern diplomatic immunity and sovereign immunity. Political matters concerning national security and associated legislation are dealt with at Westminster and not devolved to the Scottish Parliament, Welsh Assembly or Northern Ireland.

Intelligence and security

A Cabinet Intelligence and Security Committee (CISC) on which the Home Office is represented is charged with ensuring the security of the nation in the face of terrorist and similar danger as 'a first responsibility of government'. The security services (*Chapter 5*) play a vital role in providing information to underpin such deliberations. To ensure that those agencies command full public support for, and confidence in, the work they do it is important that the representatives of the people hold them to account at this level and in an appropriate manner, while respecting operational sensitivities.

The work of the security and intelligence agencies often, by its nature, involves highly-classified information, disclosure of which would be gravely damaging to the national interest and could put individuals at risk. This must be a fundamental consideration in determining the conduct of Parliamentary scrutiny if that oversight is not to undermine the operational effectiveness of the services concerned. Yet there must be effective oversight of expenditure, and administration. The CISC not only scrutinises this but has regular access to classified information and evidence; that are also normally shared with a joint Intelligence and Security Committee (ISC) made up of members of both Houses of Parliament.[23]

The Parliamentary ISC has senior and well-qualified membership drawn from all the major political parties. It has sometimes acted independently and to scrutinise the work of the agencies and other parts of the intelligence community. Its reports are published and debated in Parliament. However, the ISC meets only in private, leading some commentators to argue that the process is not sufficiently transparent. This has led to proposals for consultation on how the underlying statutory basis of the ISC might be amended and updated, in particular so as to bring the way in which its members are appointed, how it operates and the nature of its reports into line with the activities of other select

---

[22] As in the case of BAE systems; but pending possible change in this regard: *Chapter 3.*
[23] A function originally discharged by a Parliamentary Select Committee for the agencies concerned under the Intelligence Services Act 1994.

committees. Any such changes will naturally need to continue alongside safeguards with regard to highly-classified information without which effective security arrangements are unlikely to subsist at all.

While this consultation is being carried out, a number of interim changes have been suggested by the Government within existing legislation, such as:

- greater transparency over how ISC members are appointed, using similar processes of consultation between the major parties as those for select committee selection;
- giving the ISC the option of meeting in public (including, if Parliament agrees, in the chambers of the Houses of Parliament);
- that House of Commons debates on the ISC's reports be led by the chair of the ISC rather than by a Government minister, with reports being debated also in the House of Lords; and
- strengthening the secretariat to the committee, including through the appointment of an independent investigator, and making that secretariat clearly separate from the staff of the Cabinet Office.

There is a clearly overlapping agenda between the work of the Home Affairs Committee (*Chapter 1*), the Foreign Affairs Select Committee and that of the ISC; with all three touching on issues relating to counter-terrorism and security. Hence (and at the time of writing) the chair of the ISC is being invited to advise on how to maximise the effectiveness of the ISC's scrutiny role, including on the ISC's relationship to Parliament and to other relevant select committees, under existing legislation. Following consultation, the Government plans to bring forward proposals for reform.

National Security Strategy
The existing mechanisms for day-to-day security exchanges in Government are noted in *Chapter 5,* including the role of COBRA and the Joint Threat Analysis Centre (JTAC). Considerable concern has been expressed about methods of decision-making in relation to UK security, in particular with regard to the decision to go to war with Iraq in 2003, the security information upon which this appears to have been based and the Government's attempts to combat the influence of al-Qaida and Muslim extremism generally (*Chapter 5*). The Government has indicated that it is to publish a National Security Strategy setting out its approach to the range of 'security challenges and opportunities' that it faces at home and overseas; allowing it to set the framework for taking forward related issues across a range of departments and agencies, and so as to reflect changed circumstances.

To oversee the development and delivery of that strategy, and the Government's wider international, European and international development policies, the Government is to establish a National Security Committee (NSC) so as to ensure that its policies and their delivery are coordinated and appropriate to the challenges of the 21st century. It is intended that the NSC meet regularly, with the prime minister as its chair, and that it will comprise senior Cabinet colleagues from all relevant departments, supported by relevant senior officials and a secretariat within the Cabinet Office. It will also replace existing separate ministerial committees on Defence and Overseas Policy, Security and Terrorism, and Europe. The Government has indicated that it is to consult Parliament over how the strategy and its implementation can best be scrutinised.

National Community Safety Plan 2006-2009
The National Community Safety Plan (NCSP) 2006-2009 in conjunction with a National Policing Plan 2006-2009 sets out the Government's three-year priorities for community safety and explains the home secretary's priorities for the police service (see, generally, *Chapter 3*). The NCSP is updated as events unfold.[24] This update builds on the plan published last year (which incorporated the National Policing Plan 2006-2009). The Police and Justice Act 2006 removed the requirement to publish the plan, however the home secretary is still required to determine strategic priorities for England and Wales, and to publish these in the manner that he or she deems to be appropriate.

Human rights aspects of national security
The same broad human rights and associated principles apply in relation to the protection of the public generally by the state as they do concerning any other aspect of law enforcement. The appropriateness of a given response falls to be determined by what is proportionate in given circumstances; much as it must be under long-established principles of English law concerning the right of an individual citizen to use reasonable physical force to defend his or her person or property. But, quite specifically, the Human Rights Act 1998 allows any state that is a party to the European Convention On Human Rights (ECHR) to enter a derogation exempting it from certain obligations in times of war or other emergency that threatens the life of the nation. That state need not then comply with the Article of the Convention in question to the legitimate extent of the derogation. Derogations must be specific and open to review, proportionate to the threat and necessary to deal with the emergency in question. General derogations are not permitted and neither is derogation in respect of the right to life (except in so far as it arises from the lawful prosecution of war) (Article 2) or

---

[24] Hence, e.g. there was a 2007-2008 update recognising and endorsing the community safety aspects in the work of a range of agencies and services.

from prohibitions against torture (Article 3), slavery (Article 4) or retrospective penal legislation (Article 7). The UK entered certain derogations during The Troubles in Northern Ireland (*Chapter 5*). Reservations are also possible.[25] Normally, the home secretary and Home Office will be central to such events.

---

[25] Further explanation is beyond the scope of this work and readers should seek information in specialist works on human rights law.

CHAPTER 3

The Police and Policing

CHAPTER 3

The Police and Policing

The Police Reform Act 2002 contains a wide range of Home Office-related measures in relation to the police and policing extending to such matters as the administration and conduct of police authorities, police forces, chief officers of police and other people serving with or alongside the police. Police forces are also reliant on the Home Office for a substantial part of their funding and resources. The 2002 Act allows a home secretary to give certain directions to police authorities, to amend police powers via delegated legislation and in the extreme to intervene by taking over police responsibilities where those primarily responsible for day-to-day policing fail in their duties. These and related functions and powers are now central to Home Office roles in relation to public safety (*Chapter 2*), crime prevention and crime reduction (*Chapter 4*) as well as certain other police-related involvements noted in this book. But the Home Office has no direct control over how policing is carried out.[1] This chapter looks at the various kinds of police of the UK and briefly at policing: the way in which police tasks are carried out. Finally, under the heading *Prosecution of Offences*, it looks briefly at this closely related but non-Home Office task including, in outline, at the Crown Prosecution Service (CPS) and Office of the Attorney General.

THE POLICE

There is no national police force as such in the UK even though certain functions described later are carried out on a national basis. Rather there is a three way system of responsibility via 43 police authorities and police forces in England

---

[1] There strong constitutional and other arguments why policing should not be in the hands of any Government. Nonetheless some commentators see a 'police state' emerging in the UK as evidenced by excessive modern-day police powers, wide-ranging criminalisation of behaviour, the vagueness of some provisions and macho posturing. But others point to democratic processes and accountability, and, e.g. the fact that, in 2007, the MPS interviewed prime minister Tony Blair three times as a witness as well as his senior Downing Street aides (some under caution as suspects): in the so-called 'cash for honours' investigation re which the Crown Prosecution Service (CPS) (see later in the chapter) independently decided against any kind of prosecution.

and Wales such as the Metropolitan Police Service (MPS), Greater Manchester Police Service or Thames Valley Police Service.[2] According to the Home Office:

> All police forces should provide excellent service to the public, while ensuring that we all have a safe environment in which to live and work.

To a considerable degree, the policing agenda is determined by the broader policy of the Government and Home Office, due, e.g. to the home secretary's historic role as the police authority for London (until 1999) and his or her continuing close, sometimes everyday, contact with the Commissioner of the MPS or his or her senior officers (including in terms of police intelligence and information). But it is important to recognise the independent yet interdependent nature of that relationship. Chief officers of police conduct their joint dealings with government through a national membership organization, the Association of Chief Police Officers (ACPO) (below) which brings a strong influence to bear on law and order strategies. In 2006, a Home Office initiative to get police forces to amalgamate into a smaller number of larger and more regional forces was shelved, at least temporarily, when it transpired that there was small enthusiasm for this amongst chief constables or police authorities locally.

Other Home Office input includes the department's involvement in the provision of police training, and the pursuit of progress and modernisation via a National Policing Plan, National Police Improvement Agency incorporating organizations such as CENTREX, formerly the National Police Training College.[3] It is also committed to programmes of scientific and technological development of the kind described later in this chapter and in *Chapter 8*.

Police values

The home secretary is accountable to Parliament for policing matters. Early in 2007, the then home secretary Dr John Reid made an extensive statement to police representatives in which he asserted that:

> The police service is at an important crossroads. Although the service is bigger and better resourced than ever, you have never faced such a wide range of challenges. And while I am proud of the Government's record investment in the service, I am also the first to admit that resources will be significantly tighter in the future. Tough choices and clear priorities will be needed. I want to take the opportunity to sum up the mission, values, goals and aspirations that I see as essential to successful policing. You will know better than I that many of the values are enduring ones ... But the

---

[2] There are further forces in Scotland and a Police Service of Northern Ireland (which replaced the former and controversial Royal Ulster Constabulary (RUC). Most items described in this chapter have their Scottish or Northern Irish equivalent.

[3] Formerly aka Bramshill Police College and still centred at Bramshill, Hampshire.

context in which the service operates has changed rapidly ... The time is right, therefore, for us to set out what you can expect from Government and what the public can expect from you. This is relevant to all ranks and grades of police personnel. The job you do in protecting and serving the public is vital for the safety of individuals and the health of society. As always, it calls for commitment, sound judgement, fairness, ingenuity, compassion, resilience and bravery ... The mission of the police service remains to protect and reassure the public, to prevent and reduce crime, to maintain order and to bring criminals to justice. The challenges have seldom been so great: from anti-social behaviour at a very local level to new developments in terrorism and organized crime on the national and international stage.

Dr Reid continued by saying that new challenges would require new approaches and working methods of the kind described in other parts of this chapter but also by stressing the need for independence from the Home Office:

It falls to the police service to deliver neighbourhood policing that is accessible and responsive to local people's priorities, while at the same time meeting the threat from serious crime and terrorism ... Neither task can or should be downgraded ... We will continue to initiate legislation where necessary, resource the police service, be open about police performance and set a smaller number of national priorities. But we will also adopt a more strategic role with less interference in the tactical issues that ought to be the business of you, the professionals ... Indeed, we need to develop a stronger sense of accountability at the most local level to deliver the service that neighbourhoods want ... Chief officers must continue to exercise their operational independence free from government interference and help guard – as must we all – the fairness and impartiality of law-enforcement ... Every police officer and member of police staff must be animated by the sense of service to the public and policing must always be rooted in our shared, core values.

Identifying certain of these core values, he emphasised that the police must be (paraphrased):

- trusted and respected everywhere: both locally and nationally, with trust being 'the bedrock of policing' and which 'generates respect';
- accountable and public facing given the fact that many police operations are hidden from public view; and
- collaborative, working in partnership with other police forces, authorities and partners to achieve things that no one police force could do alone.

Continuous improvement
Noting that the police service had already delivered significant achievements to date he stressed the need to build on this, including via: visible, responsive and accountable local policing; joint local problem-solving; the delivery of services through collaboration and partnerships; the need for local communities to help in shaping services; and for citizens to value their contact with the police. There

was a need to deliver maximum value for money; a world class capacity to deal effectively with terrorism and serious crime; 'the right people doing the right job'; a new focus on skills and leadership development; greater rewards for effective performance in the workforce; and the use and development of the latest technology (see further below and also *Chapter 8*). In return, he committed government to: fewer targets and mandates from the centre; less 'chopping and changing' of investment priorities and programmes; and less bureaucracy.[4]

Police forces and police authorities

The Metropolitan Police Service (MPS or 'Met') is the UK's largest police force and one of the biggest., most influential and - as 'Scotland Yard'[5] - best-known worldwide It was founded in 1829 under home secretary (later prime minister) Sir Robert Peel and together with the City of London Police is responsible for the policing of the whole of Greater London.[6] The MPS has faced huge policing challenges in recent times, especially due to terrorism (*Chapter 5*) and in the wake of the London bombings and the Stockwell Shooting in particular.[7] As already indicated the role of the MPS commissioner is pivotal in terms of high profile police strategy and policy.

Outside of London the police are organized via local police forces approximating to the size of a county, or sometimes covering two or more small counties.[8] Beyond this there are a number of non-geographic police forces including the British Transport Police who operate nationwide under separate legislation, and the Royal Military Police (a Ministry of Defence responsibility).

Local police authorities are made up of citizens such as magistrates, councillors and community representatives and represent the democratic side of policing at local level. Under the Police Reform Act 2002, the home secretary can,

---

[4] Paperwork and form filling are the bane of police officers' lives and matters to which police culture is opposed in contradistinction to 'getting on with the job'. Also indicative of pragmatic attitudes, *The Job* is a leading journal for rank and file officers.

[5] From the name of the original MPS headquarters, close to London's Embankment. They are still called 'Scotland Yard' but at are located at Broadway, London SW1H 0BG. See, generally, www.met.police.uk

[6] It employs over 25,000 police officers and 10,000 civilians. The British Transport Police also has a major presence in the capital.

[7] A seminal event in the history of UK policing, the ramifications of which continue: the shooting dead at Stockwell London Underground Station by armed police of a Brazilian man, John Charles de Menezes in mistake for a terrorist in 2005; the day after a series of unsuccessful attempts to detonate bombs across the transport system; and two weeks after the London bombings of July 7 with security services on full alert during what according to the MPS was 'the biggest operation of its kind ever mounted in the UK'.

[8] As, e.g. with Devon and Cornwall, or Thames Valley Police (an amalgam of Berkshire, Buckinghamshire and Oxfordshire).

subject to certain pre-conditions, issue directions to a police authority in the interests of the effective and efficient administration of its functions with regard to policing in its area. There is an influential national Association of Police Authorities (APA) which describes itself as 'the national voice for police authorities in England, Wales and Northern Ireland' and that seeks to 'influence policy on policing'. The APA was established in 1997 to represent police authorities, both in the national arena and locally. Dr. Reid, in his statement noted earlier, describing the Home Office role in relation to policing, said:

> We work with chief police officers and police authorities … to manage police forces … A three-way system of responsibility ensures forces run smoothly … We fund the police and have overall responsibility as overseer and coordinator … chief police officers have responsibility for the direction and control of regional forces … Police authorities make sure local forces operate efficiently and effectively … This system prevents political interference in policing and avoids giving any single organization power over the entire police service …

He added that the Home Office will continue to be accountable to Parliament for policing nationally, 'intervening locally only as a last resort where a serious issue has arisen and other local steps have failed to have an effect'; and also that 'police authorities will ensure that forces have the resources, the performance framework and the appropriate local priorities to meet local people's expectations and to hold them to account for delivery'.

Police officers, special constables and police community support officers

There are some 143,000 police officers, 13,000 volunteer special constables and 7,000 police community support officers (PCSOs) in England and Wales. Provisions exist within the Police Reform Act 2002 for chief constables to authorise civilians to carry out certain police functions.[9]

Police officers of whatever rank are known as 'constables': from the chief constable (the head of each local force) downwards via their deputies, assistants, superintendents, inspectors, sergeants and rank and file basic grade police officers. Most police powers such as those of arrest and detention are conferred on police constables in general unless (e.g. as with the supervision of police custody suites or extended forms of detention under the Police and Criminal Evidence Act 1984 (known as PACE)) statutory authority is restricted to certain levels of senior officer. Police officers may operate in uniform or plain clothes (as a Criminal Investigation Department (CID) or nowadays as the nationwide Serious and Organized Crime Agency (SOCA)(below).

---

[9] See sections 38-47 of the 2002 Act. These are of a potentially ground-breaking nature.

Special constables are part-time police officers who work on a voluntary basis providing a public service alongside regular, full-time, police officers. Although supported and supervised, they have the same legal powers as their full-time colleagues and sometimes provide a vital resource where large numbers of police officers are required at a given place or event.

By way of an innovation, police community support officers, PCSOs were deployed in London from 2002 initially as part of a Home Office-led initiative to ensure greater visibility in policing (sometimes called 'reassurance policing); at first in 'crime hot spots' to deter crime, disorder and anti-social behaviour (ASB). Under the Police Reform Act 2002, PCSOs were given powers to detain people for up to 30 minutes pending the arrival of a police officer proper (but not to arrest them), and to issue fixed penalties for a range of ASB such as drunkenness, dropping litter and writing graffiti. These powers have been extended incrementally and PCSOs, whilst initially viewed with some suspicion by police officers,[10] now play a key role in relation to policing on the streets of the UK and in establishing links with neighbourhoods. They do not have powers of arrest, cannot interview or deal with prisoners, can only investigate minor offences and do not carry out more complex or high-risk tasks that police officers perform. But, as with police officers, PCSOs fall within the remit of the Independent Police Complaints Commission (IPCC) (see *Scrutiny of the Police*: below).

The Association of Chief Police Officers (ACPO)
ACPO is an independent, professionally led strategic policing body whose members come from the senior ranks of the police, including chief constables, their deputies, assistant chief constables and commanders (a rank unique to the MPS), sometimes collectively know as 'ACPO ranks'. It seeks to operate in the public interest and via active partnership with Government and the Association of Police Authorities (APA) above; leading and coordinating the direction and development of the police service in England, Wales and Northern Ireland. In times of national need ACPO - on behalf of all chief officers - coordinates strategic policing responses. ACPO's objectives include 'to provide strong and visible leadership ... inspiring confidence in those we lead, our partners and the diverse communities we serve' and 'to ensure, with our partners, that the development of doctrine for the service is conducted in a professional and coordinated manner, supporting the continuous improvement of policing for the benefit of the communities that we serve. ACPO has adopted the Nolan Principles as its Code of Ethics and Statement of Values.[11] ACPO Also represents

---

[10] Hence, e.g. the term 'plastic policemen'; and also 'hobby-bobby' for special constable.

[11] These, 'The Seven Principles of Public Life', are: *Selflessness* (holders of public office should take decisions solely in terms of the public interest; and not in order to gain financial or other material benefits for themselves, their family, or friends); *Integrity*

its members in negotiations over such matters as pay and conditions of service. The Police Superintendent's Association and Police Federation have a comparable representative and negotiating role in relation to other police ranks.

SOME SPECIALIST AREAS OF POLICING

Police forces frequently have their own specialist units or squads, e.g. focusing on drugs, burglary, vehicle crime, sexual offences or anti-social behaviour. Various national police bodies emerged to deal with certain matters at a higher level, that are now the subject of a National Policing Plan (below) as a result of which some of the most significant developments in policing to occur for decades have taken place during the past few years including the examples that follow.

The Serious and Organized Crime Agency (SOCA)
SOCA was launched in 2006 under the Serious Organised Crime and Police Act 2005.[12] Its aim is 'to reduce the harm caused to the UK by serious organized crime'; estimated at over £20 billion a year. SOCA brought together the former National Crime Squad (NCS), National Criminal Intelligence Service (NCIS) and their associated databases and those parts of HM Revenue and Customs that dealt with drug-trafficking and criminal finance and of the then UK Immigration Service (now part of the Border and Immigration Agency: *Chapter 6*) that dealt with organized immigration crime (including, e.g. 'people trafficking'). A key SOCA responsibility is dealing with financial information in relation to the suspected proceeds of crime and money laundering; a function that it took over from the Assets Recovery Agency formed under the Proceeds of Crime Act 2002. Increasingly, highly sophisticated ways of tracing transactions have led to the seizure of property and funds.[13] In straightforward terms, it has been asserted by

---

(they should not place themselves under any financial or other obligation to outside individuals or organizations that might influence them in the performance of their official duties); *Objectivity* (in carrying out public business, including making public appointments, awarding contracts, or recommending individuals for rewards and benefits, they should make choices on merit); *Accountability* (for their decisions and actions to the public and they must submit themselves to whatever scrutiny is appropriate to their office); *Openness* (they should be as open as possible about all the decisions and actions that they take and give reasons for their decisions and restrict information only when the wider public interest clearly demands it); *Honesty* (they have a duty to declare any private interests relating to their public duties and to take steps to resolve any conflicts arising in a way that protects the public interest); and *Leadership* (they should promote and support these principles by leadership and example).

[12] Also known as SOCAP.

[13] Even if the procedures have sometime been laborious and subject to legal challenges.

ministers on several occasions that a function of SOCA was to 'harry, hassle and hound' offenders suspected of involvement in such dealings.

SOCA is an executive non-departmental public body (NDPB) sponsored by, but operationally independent from, the Home Office. It is led by a board with a majority of non-executive members. The board is responsible for ensuring that SOCA discharges its statutory responsibilities and meets strategic priorities set by the home secretary. The director general of SOCA is responsible for all that SOCA does operationally and administratively, as well as for day-to-day management, including expenditure. Under the 2005 Act, SOCA must publish an annual plan before the start of each financial year and an annual report as soon as possible after the end of each financial year.[14]

'SOCA Online' is a secure system designed for use by those people and entities who must, under the, Proceeds of Crime Act 2002 and the Terrorism Act 2000 submit 'Suspicious Activity Reports (SARs)' to SOCA. These target such criminal proceeds via, e.g. banks, lawyers, accountants and businesses who may, e.g. encounter money laundering when dealings with clients or customers. This has been enhanced by provisions that allow any police officer to seize cash above a statutory amount[15] in the absence of a satisfactory explanation for carrying it; and associated Crown Prosecution Service (CPS) procedures. SOCA would also appear to have superseded Special Branch except in the context that such 'branches' still sometimes exist locally: see the further comments in *Chapter 5*.

The Child Exploitation and Online Protection Centre (CEOP)

CEOP works across the UK and maximises international links to tackle child sex abuse wherever and whenever it happens. Part of CEOP's strategy for achieving this is by providing internet safety advice for parents and carers and delivering a virtual police station for reporting abuse on the internet. CEOP grew out of a number of earlier initiatives including Operation Ore that from 2002 onwards targeted some 7,000 people suspected of downloading child pornography from the internet. CEOP works in both online and offline environments to protect children from sexual exploitation. The CEOP Centre is affiliated to SOCA (above) and powers are derived from the Serious Organised Crime and Police Act 2005. It is based in Pimlico, London with developing outreach channels to all areas of both domestic and international policing. Within SOCA (above), there are also separate arrangements covering operations, intelligence, education and victim identification. SOCA is a member of the Virtual Global Taskforce (VGT) whose

---

[14] SOCA annual plans can be viewed at www.soca.gov.uk
[15] Initially £10,000 or more; but now £5,000 or more; under section 294 of the 2002 Act and subject to police codes of procedure.

members include the Australian Federal Police, US Immigration and Customs Enforcement, Royal Canadian Mounted Police and Interpol.[16]

Other specialist tasks

Other specialist police responsibilities exist within local police forces to deal with such matters as local drug or alcohol problems, shoplifting, football related violence and the policing of sports grounds,[17] weapons, and road traffic matters. Each also has its own specially trained firearms officers. Crime prevention and crime reduction are dealt with in *Chapter 4*; terrorism in *Chapter 5*; and the Forensic Science Service (FSS) and scenes of crime officers (SOCOs) in *Chapter 8*.

POLICING

As already indicated at the start of this chapter, 'policing' denotes ways, methods, styles, types or approaches to carrying out the police role, whether of an overall strategic kind or directed to an individual event, situation or area of policing, such as child protection or organized crime. Policing styles may depend on a range of factors, including the prevailing views of the chief constable of a given police area or the head of a special policing unit or police operation; but, increasingly now, there is the influential National Policing Plan (below).

Thus, e.g. community policing came to the fore from the 1970s onwards, the notion of community involvement or influence in the setting of policies strategies and priorities (but without any direct community involvement in operational matters); whilst 'neighbourhood policing' implies a similar but more specifically directed, two-way approach. Many commentators urge the broad need for policing by consent. In contrast, terms like 'aggressive policing' (as with riots, disturbances or terrorism), pro-active as opposed to reactive policing and 'disruptive methods' (as with organized crime) all have their place in theories of policing as do works on ethics, integrity and general principles of policing and police leadership. Various influential police texts exist in this regard some of which are listed within *Appendix IV* to this work.

National Policing Improvement Agency (NPIA)

The NPIA is a new agency created to support police forces to improve the way in which they work. It is police owned and led and replaced or incorporated former national policing organizations such as the Police Information Technology Organization (PITO) and CENTREX, as well as certain functions that were formerly carried out by the Home Office and ACPO. Its origins lay in Home

---

[16] Details are available at www.ceop.gov.uk and www.virtualglobaltaskforce.com
[17] Although in practice the latter, in many instances, involves private sector security.

Office responses to suggestions by ACPO that an agency should be established to support the implementation of national standards. The Government committed itself to establishing the NPIA in the Home Office under a five-year strategic plan (below), first published in July 2004 and updated on a rolling basis; and similarly in the police reform White Paper, *Building Communities, Beating Crime: A Better Police Service for the 21st Century*.[18] According to the Home Office, the NPIA 'will:

- look ahead to identify and plan for the future challenges to face policing;
- define the police service's capacity to implement change and inform the priority and sequence of change programmes;
- find and develop evidence-based policing good practice that works and support the service to ensure good practice is applied;
- play a lead role in ensuring that an agreed programme of key reforms takes place;
- co-ordinate the future development, purchase and deployment of nationally-compatible systems and infrastructure, particularly information and communications technology;
- design, develop, deploy and quality assure nationally-compatible learning programmes;
- help the police service to recruit, train and develop its people and improve leadership at all levels;
- ensure the workforce, processes, procurement and systems that support policing are as efficient and effective as possible;
- use research and analysis and specialist systems and advice to improve policing and provide a better service to the public;
- ensure that police forces and police authorities are involved in every aspect of the agency's work.'

As its name implies, a main focus of the work of the NPIA is improving policing in England and Wales. This it is intended to do by via a fair and equitable service to diverse communities and police staff. Its functions include enhanced coordination of major national projects previously managed by separate organizations; the rationalisation of policing agencies; and removal of duplication and waste - all matters that have tended to characterise nationwide policing functions in the past. In this, science and technology will be at the fore.

SCRUTINY OF THE POLICE

Quite apart from the democratic process under which the home secretary is accountable to Parliament for policing there are certain direct forms of scrutiny.

---

[18] (2004) Cm 6360.

Her Majesty's Inspectorate of Constabulary (HMIC)

For some 150 years now HMICs have been charged with examining and improving the efficiency of the police service, the first HMIC being appointed under the County and Borough Police Act 1856. In modern times, they are appointed by the Crown on the recommendation of the home secretary and report to HM Chief Inspector of Constabulary (HMCIC), who is also the home secretary's principal professional policing adviser. The HMCIC is independent of the Home Office and the police service. His functions include certifying police forces as efficient and thus qualified to receive a police grant. The inspectorate's role has been progressively developed over the past 30 years to be more open and transparent and to include not only the inspection of individual forces but also analysis, assessment and promoting best practice across a range of operational and professional matters.

HMIC adopts a risk-assessment approach to prioritising work, based on core objectives of: driving up police performance; providing assurance to stakeholders; making an input to Home Office policy-making; contributing to improvements to the Criminal Justice System (CJS); and providing advice and consultative support to chief constables and police authority members. Inspection reports are normally published, as is an annual business plan setting out specific priorities and targets for each current year.[19]

The Independent Police Complaints Commission (IPCC)

The IPCC became operational in 2004 under the Police Reform Act 2002 and in place of the former Police Complaints Authority (PCA) that had to an extent fallen into disrepute from its lack of any real independence from police forces; frequently being criticised as 'the police investigating the police'. The IPCC is a non-departmental public body (NDPB), funded by the Home Office, and in its present incarnation is by law entirely independent of the police, interest groups and political parties. Notably, its decisions in individual cases are free from any government or partisan involvement. The IPCC has a duty to oversee the whole of the police complaints system, as created by the 2002 Act, the main aim being to transform the way in which complaints against the police are handled and to ensure that they are dealt with effectively. Hence, the IPCC also sets standards for the way the police handle complaints and, if something does go awry, it seeks to help the police to learn lessons and improve the way in which they work.[20]

---

[19] See http://inspectorates.homeoffice.gov.uk/hmic/

[20] The IPCC's first major investigation was into the 'Stockwell Shooting' that brought it into some initial conflict with the MPS, but it subsequently absolved the Metropolitan Police commissioner of any wrongdoing, though it was critical of a senior MPS officer (see earlier footnote and also in *Chapter 5*). But readers should note that some aspects of these tragic events involve proceedings that are still ongoing and hence *sub judice.*

MODERN-DAY ADVANCES IN POLICING

Advances in science and technology are altering the way in which both the Home Office and the police work to tackle sometimes sophisticated modern-day forms of crime such as, 'cyber-crime' (a label that has been applied to a range of offences committed over the internet); and also the way in which crimes are detected or solved, especially by means of CCTV and other forms of surveillance. Some further information appears in *Chapter 8*, but it may be useful to note here in outline some of the ways in which developments in science, technology and working methods are affecting everyday policing, i.e. via:

- advanced communications systems;
- advanced forms of data sharing with other government departments, services, units, agencies and/or the private sector;
- enhanced forms of surveillance using modern day control rooms;
- internet-based investigations, including the retrieval of electronic data, e.g. from hard discs and electronic chips (including 'deleted' data);
- new and remote ways of monitoring people, traffic, animals or items, including by means of heat seeking equipment and global satellite positioning technology, especially in relation to the use of mobile telephones at a given place and time;
- the use of CCTV(including that provided by the private sector), extending now, e.g. to experiments with intelligent CCTV (talking cameras);
- the use of video recording, including current developments in relation to 'real time video analysis, cameras fitted to police vehicles and within police officers' helmets (a practice that would appear to be spreading nationwide) and the application of various forms of video footage to investigations, court proceedings and evidence;
- DNA-testing ('genetic fingerprinting') (see the extended note in *Chapter 8*);
- a range of advances and initiative in relation to drug-testing;
- facial recognition technology, often in conjunction with an electronic 'Rogues Gallery' of offenders and suspects;
- developments in biometrics, iris recognition and in the direction of identity cards (as explained in relation to border control in *Chapter 6*);
- secondary uses of speed cameras or congestion charging equipment and data (currently limited to terrorism);
- a range of developments in relation to road traffic, including instant access to databases and stinger devices to bring a vehicle to a halt; and
- modern-day forms of non-lethal force (where any such force is necessary) as well as access to specialist, rapid response firearms units when required.

All of these developments are accompanied by existing or developing codes of practice, standards and training for operators. They follow from such strategies as those noted in the 2006 Cabinet Office paper, *Building On Progress: Security, Crime and Justice*[21] which reveals the Government's proposals and ideas for confronting crime and criminals in the coming decade. That report looks, in particular, at how new technology, powers, service structures and ways of 'fighting offending' will need to keep pace with an ever changing society.

SOME CURRENT ISSUES IN POLICING

A National Policing Plan 2005-2008 was published by the Home Office following extensive consultation with the Association of Chief Police Officers (ACPO), Association of Police Authorities (APA) and other stakeholders. It highlights certain key issues facing the police service today and subsists within the wider context of a Home Office Strategic Plan 2004-08 and policy papers of the kind noted elsewhere in this book. The plan stemmed from *Building Communities, Beating Crime: A Better Police Service for the 21st Century*.[22] That White Paper spoke of the need for further reform and for collaboration with other departments and services within a national framework.

An independent assessment
A few years on there are, it is suggested, four main issues that are likely to concern policing in the first decade of the 21st century. The first is the structure of the police service itself and of its accountability to government, Parliament, its stakeholders and the public. There are important and related questions about its authority and legitimacy in a society where policing is by consent. National concerns and priorities concerning terrorism and organized crime need to be balanced with local community concerns over low level crime, public disorder and anti-social behaviour – concerns that will vary considerably from place-to-place. Associated questions relate to the role of central and local government in influencing police practice, and to the functions and powers of police authorities, including the case for an element of direct election.

A second issue concerns *what the police should actually do*, and the powers, equipment and technology they should have to do it. The answer may seem obvious if it is in simple terms of preventing crime and arresting criminals. It is less obvious how far the police should be concerned with behaviour that is not actually criminal or people who may be potential offenders but who are not suspected of any offence (as noted in *Chapter 4* when describing the legal status

---

[21] (2006) Cabinet Office/Prime Minister's Strategy Unit. Ref: 280238/0307/D2.4
[22] Cm 6360.

of anti-social behaviour (ASB)), or whether, e.g. the police should have a presence in schools and colleges. Nor is it obvious how far the police should have further powers of summary justice such as on-the-spot fines, or further powers to arrest and the right to question suspects or detain them for longer without trial (see, in particular, *Chapter 5*), or what rules should apply to the use of such powers if they were made available.

A third issue is the relationship between policing by 'regular' or 'sworn' police officers and the activities of other people who carry out policing functions, such as PCSOs (above), traffic wardens, private sector security guards or other people who may in future be authorised to do so by chief constables under the Police Reform Act 2002 (above). One question is whether such activities should continue to grow and be encouraged; another is whether more police functions should be 'contracted out' if the private sector can perform them as effectively; and another, again, is whether such activities should be brought within a more systematic framework of regulation, accountability and control.

The fourth issue is sometimes called 'workforce modernisation', and arises from the complaint that the police have successfully resisted all attempts, by successive governments over the past 25 years, to reform the police service. Modernisation might involve changes in conditions of service, training and career progression, and in the arrangements for recruitment, promotion, retirement and discipline.[23] Perhaps a main aim should be to create a police service which would be more versatile, qualified, diverse and flexible, with a wider range of backgrounds, skills, experience and expertise.

THE PROSECUTION OF OFFENCES

Prosecution is not a Home Office or government function albeit that confusion sometimes exists with regard to the legitimate role of the attorney general which has come under the spotlight in modern times due to the perceived conflicts of interest that are inherent in that role.

The Office of the Attorney General

Certain other chapters refer to the key trilateral arrangement whereby the home secretary, Lord Chancellor and attorney general are at the centre of strategic decision making with regard to criminal policy and strategy. The role of the attorney general (AG) is some five centuries old. He or she[24] is the Crown's chief law officer who tenders his or her advice in complex situations to the government, to which he or she is chief legal adviser. He or she also supervises

---

[23] Some such provisions appear in the Police Reform Act 2002.
[24] The first woman attorney general, Baroness Scotland QC, was appointed in 2007.

both of the two main public prosecuting agencies in England and Wales, the Crown Prosecution Service (CPS) and the Serious Fraud Office (SFO); and may be involved in decisions whether or not to prosecute someone in a difficult case of murder, or one that involves national security and, especially, in modern times, terrorism. Certain prosecutions require his or her consent, or fiat. There is also a general 'public interest' duty, an example of which is that to appeal to the Court of Appeal against what the AG considers to be 'unduly lenient sentences'. The AG's department is not part of the Home Office (nor of the Ministry of Justice (MOJ)), but is closely allied as a partner within the trilateral arrangement already referred to. The Government has, alongside a more wide ranging review of constitutional affairs, said that it will look at certain criticisms that have arisen and that ahead of any resulting changes the AG will no longer be involved in a range of sensitive areas. These will also be examined within the context of an MOJ Green Paper, *The Governance of Britain*.[25]

The Crown Prosecution Service (CPS)
Most day-to-day prosecution functions do not reach the more rarified atmosphere of the Office of the Attorney General but are discharged by the CPS. The prosecution function has been a CPS responsibility since the formation of that service in 1986 under the Prosecution of Offences Act 1985. It replaced a variable collection of directly police-linked 'prosecuting solicitors' within or attached to local police forces. Previously, cases were prosecuted by the police themselves, often by a 'prosecuting inspector', or even the arresting officer.[26] Post-Criminal Justice Act 2003, the CPS takes full responsibility for most police-related decisions about who is to be charged and with what offence.

The CPS is led by the director of public prosecutions (DPP) who reports to the AG (who is accountable to Parliament for its work).[27] It consists of Crown prosecutors of various ranks (as well as administrative staff). The DPP must issue a code for the guidance of CPS staff; a public document containing, e.g. advice on prosecution decision-making, setting out factors to be taken into account and a twin evidential and public interest tests (is there enough evidence and does the public interest justify prosecution).[28] CPS headquarters are in London and York and its overall structure coincides with police force areas. Often there is local Criminal Justice Unit (CJU) in which CPS and police administrative staff work alongside one another with a view to efficient preparation of case files.

[25] (2007) Cm 7170. Some further information appears in *The New Ministry of Justice*.
[26] The further back in time, the more likely that this was the case – although the practice persisted in areas of London into the late-20th century. The long redundant terms 'police court' and 'police prosecutor' serve as reminders of these former times.
[27] The main CPS office is at 50 Ludgate Hill, London EC4M 7EX; www.cps.gov.uk
[28] Special considerations apply to juveniles.

Crime Prevention
and Crime Reduction

CHAPTER 4

Crime Prevention and Crime Reduction

Increasingly over the past 25 years the *prevention* of crime – and more particularly the *reduction* of crime – has become a priority on the Home Office and wider political agenda. These objectives are now reflected across the wider Criminal Justice System (CJS) in the aims, objectives and mission statements of departments, services, charities and other organizations: hence, also, common self-descriptions such as 'crime prevention agency' and 'crime reduction charity'. These twin objectives are as central, e.g. to the work of the police, HM Prison Service (HMPS) and the National Probation Service (NPS) as they are to the Ministry of Justice (MOJ)[1] and non-statutory sector organizations such as the National Council for the Care and Resettlement of Offenders (Nacro) and Crime Concern. Much is also achieved by the private sector and the security industry.

Crime prevention and crime reduction bear different nuances and emphases. Preventing crime serves to reduce it. Crime reduction implicitly recognises that it may not be possible to prevent every criminal offence so that a lesser and more realistic aim is preferable. People may not be caught or deterred by every crime prevention measure but it *is* possible to make a difference as regards overall crime levels via a range of strategies. Both objectives can be tackled on a broad front, e.g. by improving policing (*Chapter 3*); imprisonment for public protection (IPP);[2] rehabilitation programmes such as those aimed at anger management, sex offending and burglary; regeneration of run-down areas; projects for people at-risk of falling into crime; and initiatives to tackle drug supply, drug and alcohol misuse and other types of crime and anti-social behaviour (ASB).

TACKLING CRIME AND THE CAUSES OF CRIME

The Home Office asserts that the risk of becoming a victim of crime is falling:

> In 1995 the risk was 40 per cent but by 2005 it had fallen to 23 per cent[3] ... But we aim to reduce this level even further. And to reduce fear of crime which has risen, despite the drop in crime. For instance, only 3.2 per cent of households become victims of burglary, but 13 per cent live in fear of it.[4]

---

[1]   As with other CJS organizations, this is affirmed at its web-site: www.justice.gov.uk
[2]   Sometimes called sentences for public protection (SPPs).
[3]   The lowest level since the *British Crime Survey* began in 1981: Report on *Crime in England and Wales* 2005/2006, Home Office.
[4]   http://www.homeoffice.gov.uk/crime-victims/reducing-crime/ Ironically, whilst seeking to reduce crime it has also been creating countless new offences: *Chapter 10*.

It proposes different responses for different types of crime and offers tips on what people can do to help combat and prevent crime as well as details about how the department has been tackling a range of scenarios:

- alcohol-related crime
- burglary
- business and retail crime
- community safety
- domestic violence
- drug-related crime
- football disorder
- fraud
- gun crime

- hate crime
- internet crime
- organized crime
- prostitution
- robbery
- sexual offences
- vehicle crime
- violent crime
- youth crime

Thus, e.g. under burglary and as a form of reassurance, it is noted that domestic burglary fell by 20 per cent in2004-2005, down to 756,000 cases and that the risk of being a victim of domestic burglary has halved since 1995.[5] It urges 'working together' as being essential to combat burglary, including partnerships with companies, theft prevention messages and the coding of property. It notes that the Government has introduced a minimum sentence of at least three years imprisonment for people convicted of burglary on three separate occasions.[6] More generally, the Home Office asserts that

> Fifty per cent of all crime is committed by just ten per cent of offenders. And the 5,000 most active offenders in the country are estimated to be responsible for a staggering one in ten offences[7] ... So if we manage to tackle this minority group of offenders, we can considerably reduce crime levels. Our Prolific and other Priority Offenders Programme aims to do just that by targeting the most prolific offenders and young offenders who are at risk of becoming part of this group ... The programme is making an impact across all crimes, especially robbery, vehicle crime and domestic burglary – in 2006 we helped 1,750 prolific offenders stop or significantly reduce their offending.[8]

Crime and Disorder Reduction Partnerships (CDRPs)

The Crime and Disorder Act 1998 required CDRPs to be set up in local areas. These bring together various interested parties including the police, local

---

[5] *Crime in England and Wales 2004/2005* (2005), Nicholas, S, Povey, D and Walker A, Home Office (11/05).

[6] Despite a general fall, detractors are quick stress that serious violent crime has been rising overall and claim that statistics can be manipulated to support political policy (*Chapter 8*); something that, if correct, the Government has now said it will put right.

[7] *Criminal Justice: The Way Ahead* (2001), Cm 5074.

[8] The significance of much of this is contested by some commentators. Much depends on as yet uncharted understanding and analysis of the 'turn over' of these active offenders.

authorities, the (now) National Probation Service (NPS), health authorities, voluntary sector, businesses and community representatives to create their own strategies to tackle crime and disorder. CDRPs seek to reduce crime and disorder in an area by, e.g.:

- establishing actual levels of crime and disorder in a given area;
- consulting widely with the population of the area to make sure that the CDRP's perceptions match those of local people, including minority or especially vulnerable groups, such as gay men and lesbians, or members of racial or religious minorities; and
- devising a package of strategic measures to tackle those problems which are identified as priorities.

This may, e.g. involve target setting and mission statements. CDRP strategies usually last for three years, but they are kept under constant review by the partnership itself. The first such strategies were published in 1999 by the then 375 partnerships that implemented them. A second CDRP round was completed in 2002, and from that time forward an extensive programme of research, training, seminars and consultancy support has been put in place by the Home Office to help partnerships in achieving 'real and sustained crime reduction'.

Social exclusion
The term 'social exclusion' describes, e.g. people or geographical locations that are barred from the opportunities that exist more widely across society because of a range of negative factors. These may include such things as high unemployment, low incomes, poor housing, bad health, widespread family breakdown, homelessness and a lack of decent community resources. Theories that 'sink estates' or areas with 'broken windows' are more prone to high crime rates are nothing new.[9] Such sentiments came to the fore in the UK in 1997 and more recently within the Government's Respect Agenda (see *Crime and Anti-social Behaviour* later in this chapter). Similar theories run in parallel so that it is broadly acknowledged that physically excluding someone from society by sending them to prison where this is not wholly necessary can have a damaging

---

[9] Often attributed to the American criminologists, James Q. Wilson and George Kelling who argued that crime, fear of crime and the acceptance of poor levels of law and order and law enforcement are more likely to occur in badly kept areas where, literally or metaphorically, windows get broken and remain so; thus leading to a lack of respect, esteem and care. 'Broken Windows' (1982), *Atlantic Monthly*. A conference focused on 'broken windows' and 'situational crime prevention' at Bramshill Police College in 1982 and a new unit was created within the Police Department at the Home Office to pursue it as a serious aspect of policy. Situational crime theories can be traced back to the work of Jane Jacobs and others and for 50 some years: see *Crime, State and Citizen, Chapter 18*.

effect on them and potential future victims - and create a growing underclass. Contrary views are less charitable or understanding and it is hard at times to reconcile the Government's existing history of 'talking tough' (that may now be partially tempered) and the record prison populations that have existed over the past ten years with some of its forward looking efforts and sentiments.

Virtually as soon as New Labour came to power in 1997, a Social Exclusion Unit (SEU) was established by prime minister Tony Blair to explore 'joined up solutions to joined up problems'. The SEU continues to work across government departments in terms both of research and the implementation and promotion of policies to confront social exclusion and poverty. From 2001, the SEU became a responsibility of the Cabinet Office and in conjunction with the Home Office and other government departments began a large scale programme of research into the causes of crime, including various aspects of social exclusion. This led to the report, *Reducing Re-offending by Ex-prisoners,*[10] a main theme of which was that imprisonment does not in itself succeed in turning the majority of offenders away from crime. It can make matters worse and frequently does so. Rather, the real key to crime reduction is to resolve the underlying causes of crime. The premise was that seven Government departments should forge a 'united front' against re-offending; with imprisonment being used only as a last resort.

Stopping offending

Social causes of crime apart, tackling crime rests upon the broad idea that potential offenders can be stopped from offending either by policing them or by punishing them where policing fails. The crime prevention debate has stretched from the primitive approaches of the Anglo-Saxon blood feud, the early 'watches' mounted around town settlements at night and other times of fear, and the use of draconian punishment based on notions of deterrence[11] through various cycles and eras when differing approaches have been attempted, to the more modern (though in some senses deeply traditional) and symbolic ones involving restorative justice, the shaming of offenders and the view that the main priority of criminal justice should be to repair the harm done to the victim and the community at large.[12] In other words, tackling crime, by whatever means, is

---

[10] (2002) Social Exclusion Unit. See www.cabinetoffice.gov.uk/social_exclusion_task_force

[11] Seemingly, those crime prevention theories based purely on notions of deterrent sentencing stand discredited. A long time exponent of this is Professor Andrew Ashworth of Oxford University. See, also, *Criminal Deterrence and Sentence Severity* (1999), Hirsh, A, Bottoms, A, Burney, E and Wikstrom, P, Hart Publishing.

[12] See, e.g. *Justice for Victims and Offenders* (2006), Wright, M, Waterside Press and other examples noted in *Appendix IV*. With the same kind of dichotomy that has attached to the social exclusion/punishment debate (see earlier footnote) the Home Office has backed restorative justice whilst introducing increasingly wide and potentially punitive

central to what any CJS is about: dealing with issues of public safety, protection of citizens and their property and maintaining law and order in general. Much rests on doing things of a practical nature, matters of good sense, following good advice and keeping to safe routines on the assumption that there are some people 'out there' who will take advantage of any lapses in security.

The Home Office

Home Office or other Government-led initiatives have targeted 'crime sensitive' planning consents by local authorities, cyber-crime (see also *Chapters 3* and *8*), mobile telephones, business and retail crime and garden crime. The Home Office looks to a range of participants, including:

- the police through their visible presence, actions against law-breakers and their reputation in terms of targeting and catching offenders;
- local communities via a range of initiatives such as improving street lighting to crime-free planning;
- voluntary organizations by proving advice, encouragement and support;
- the private sector that may decide to install surveillance and detection schemes out of self-interest; and
- self-help such as that which flows from Neighbourhood Watch, Business Watch, Vehicle Watch, Boat Watch, Farm Watch and similar schemes.

To an extent and in relation to what might be termed run-of-the-mill crime the role of the Home Office is to facilitate and support other crime prevention initiatives, including developments in relation to terrorism (*Chapter 5*), border controls (*Chapter 6*) and applied science or technology (*Chapter 8*). Some strategies for the protection of the public and national security of the kind alluded to in *Chapter 2* have an inbuilt crime prevention/reduction effect. It is also likely that in policing greater problems many lesser ones may incidentally come to be resolved in that process. Key Home Office arrangements include:

- an Office for Security and Counter-Terrorism, that works in partnership with other departments and agencies to ensure a more effective and co-ordinated response to threats to UK security (*Chapters 1* and *5*);
- a Crime Reduction and Community Safety Group, that seeks to deliver results via the police service and its partners (*Chapter 3*);
- a Respect Task Force, which works across government to tackle the causes of anti-social behaviour, 'which lie in families, in the classroom and in communities' (see *Crime and Anti-social Behaviour*, below);

---

criminal justice legislation. The modern world is sometimes perhaps too fast moving for over-indulgence in progressive ideas and longer term thinking.

- a small strategic centre, that advises the Home Office board on overall strategy and direction and the allocation of resources; and
- professional services, including legal advice, analysis and communications support, and programme and project management support.

Wider crime prevention/reduction strategies include combining information about offending with that about fear of crime and statistics designed to reassure citizens that most crime is on the decrease.[13] The Home Office also offers its own practical advice of which the following are examples:

> Many of the steps suggested here are common sense, but they can make a real difference to your safety. By securing your home and property you can save yourself the distress and expense of crime, and make your community a safer and better place to live ... A burglar only needs to spot an open window, unlocked side gate or dodgy alarm to make their move. Think about it – if you know your home security looks poor, so will a thief ... Many crimes are as simple as an opportunity exploited. Don't give thieves that chance.

> Protect your home .... Having the right doors, windows and locks can make your home safer ... Stay safe on public transport ... Take a few actions to ensure that your journey is a safe one ... Stop vehicle crime ... Keep your vehicle safe with our handy crime prevention tips ... Bogus callers ... Don't fall victim to bogus callers - keep them outside ... Telephone scams ... When the offer is too good to be true - hang up on them! ... Mark your property ... A few simple actions can help you get your property back after a crime. [14]

Most local police forces have their own crime reduction websites offering a broad range of advice to local citizens often in response to a particular spate of offending. Tagging of property whether by electronic means or other forms of identification is a service often offered free of charge; whilst police forces regularly conduct high profile 'blitzes', 'crackdowns' and seek to encourage new scientific developments such as 'SmartWater', noted in the next section.

The voluntary, non-statutory sector and private sector

Shelter, the housing charity, is just one example of a charitable organization that proffers advice to people seeking to safeguard their homes:

> Make sure that all the doors and windows to your property have adequate locks - and make sure you always lock up before you go out! ... Doors should be fitted with a five lever mortice lock and windows should fasten with a key, which must then be

---

[13] *Chapter 8.* Despite an escalating prison population: as to which, for some further information, see the companion to this work, *The New Ministry of Justice.*

[14] www.crimereduction.gov.uk

kept out of sight. However, make sure everyone in your home knows where the keys are kept in case of an emergency such as a fire. Doors and door and window frames should be strong and in good condition, so they can't be broken easily. You could also consider fitting: a chain on the door; a spy hole; an alarm ... If you live in rented accommodation and don't feel the property is sufficiently secure, ask your landlord to fit new or additional locks.

This advice continues by advising people to fit locks and security devices, keep valuables out of sight, use entry phone systems in flats, etc., join Neighbourhood Watch, take precautions when going away, beware bogus callers and 'think about what's outside such as ladders that might be used by a burglar or keys under the mat or in other obvious places'. Shelter is supported by Government grants and sponsorship from the private sector.[15] Amongst the many other nationwide bodies involved in crime prevention/reduction are the BBC (both through its regular and long running and seemingly, generally well-regarded, *Crimewatch* programme and at various BBC web-sites[16] and Crimestoppers, an independent UK-wide charity 'working to stop crime' that can be called on the telephone anonymously.[17]

As to the private sector, many businesses or private sector financed organizations operate in this field, including the Joseph Rowntree Foundation, as well as security firms and those marketing CCTV and other forms of surveillance (*Chapters 3* and *8*). SmartWater is a police accredited venture which has developed modern-day, often scientific, crime reduction programmes for law enforcement agencies worldwide that, so it claims, have been proven to reduce crimes such as burglary and auto-crime, by over 80 per cent in some instances. SmartWater strategy involves training police officers and police community support officers (*Chapter 3*) to use its forensic products. These include a coded liquid for security marking of personal property that employs DNA-based methods 'in a way that creates fear and anxiety within the criminal fraternity'.[18]

An example of a crime prevention and crime reduction strategy
Practical examples of crime prevention/reduction are to be found in the approaches to public safety and public protection that are described in *Chapter 2*. One development has been proactive policing through the creation of lists and databases and, in the case of sex offenders, the sex offender order and Sex Offender Register. This also links to the work of Multi-agency Protection Panels (MAPPAs) described in that chapter. The sex offender order is an order of a criminal court, first introduced by the Crime and Disorder Act 1998 that police or

---

[15] Crime prevention advice www.england.shelter.uk.org is sponsored by Vodafone.

[16] See, e.g. www.bbc.co.uk/learning/subjects/legal

[17] 0800 555 111. See, also, www.crimestoppers-uk.org

[18] Hence the verb 'to SmartWater'. See www.smartwater.com

prosecutors can apply for in respect of any such offender whose behaviour in the community gives reasonable cause for concern in relation to the protection of the public from serious harm. It can be made on application to a magistrates' court (under its civil jurisdiction) and requires the person named in it to register under with the police whilst the order is in effect. It is a criminal offence to break the terms of such an order which is now also made as a matter of course whenever someone is convicted of any one of a range of scheduled sexual offences.[19]

CRIME AND ANTI-SOCIAL BEHAVIOUR

Preventing and reducing crime now extends to preventative measures designed to tackle anti-social behaviour (ASB). Preventive justice is nothing new. Its origins go back to the Justice of the Peace Act 1361 and the power of magistrates to bind over people to keep the peace and be of good behaviour. Some vagueness about what was meant by 'good behaviour' caused that power to stall post-Human Rights Act 1998, but it is still extant and correctly used by the courts, after more than 650 years. Its so-called 'smart justice' modern-day counterpart is the anti-social behaviour order (ASBO), which is possibly more easily used and certainly more significant in its potential impact.

Criminal responsibility attaches only when a criminal offence is committed, such as theft, burglary, driving with excess alcohol in the blood, murder, rape or indecent assault. There is a fundamental divide between criminal and civil responsibility. Historically, for the latter, purely private remedies were normally sought in the civil courts. Criminal proceedings are hedged about with special rules of procedure and evidence. The ingredients of such offences are strictly defined and, if the accused person pleads 'not guilty', they must be proved by evidence to a high standard of proof, beyond reasonable doubt. The protection afforded by human rights law is also far greater when considering criminal responsibility; and codes, standards and procedures operate at a substantially higher level all round. The schism between civil and criminal proceedings is well-illustrated by the anti-social behaviour order (ASBO) which, despite some outward appearances is civil, not criminal, in type.[20] Civil matters do not ordinarily attract penal sanctions in the sense of punishment. Breach of an ASBO *is* a crime; one that is punishable in the Crown Court by a maximum of five years

---

[19] The national sex offender register is maintained by the police (and draws together information from entries made by local sex offender registrars of local police forces). The provisions are retrospective re, e.g. existing prisoners.

[20] A differently constructed and legally quite different criminal anti-social behaviour (or CRASBO) that a court may attach to a sentence is by contrast criminal in nature.

imprisonment in the case of an adult (two years for a juvenile) and/or an unlimited fine.[21]

The ASBO is thus a new hybrid system of law enforcement[22] in which civil standards apply at the outset, when an ASBO is being sought, but criminal sanctions exist if an ASBO is breached. Criticisms have thus attached to it, various commentators noting that it 'short circuits' the criminal process and risks criminalising people who may only be guilty of nuisance-type behaviour. Nonetheless, since 1997 the ASBO has become one of the flagships of Home Office crime prevention/crime reduction policies.[23]

Respect, crime prevention and crime reduction

ASBOs were first introduced by the Crime and Disorder Act 1998, but, seemingly spurred on by their general popularity, their scope was extended by the Police Reform Act 2002 and Anti-social Behaviour Act 2003. They can now be used in relation to a child over ten years of age and adults who have behaved 'in an anti-social manner that caused or was likely to cause harassment, alarm or distress' and where they are 'necessary to protect other people from further anti-social acts'. According to the Home Office:[24]

> Despite a 39% drop in the incidence of crime since 1995, anti-social behaviour remains a serious issue with around 66,000 reports of ASB made to authorities each day ... We are making progress, however. The number of people who think ASB is a big or fairly big problem has reduced from 20.7 per cent in 2002/03 to 16.7 per cent at the end of 2004 but there still is much more we can be doing together to tackle the problem. (Source: British Crime Survey)

The government's Respect Agenda noted in relation to social exclusion earlier in this chapter, its Respect Action Plan and associated arrangements and court powers such as the dispersal order, acceptable behaviour contracts and individual support orders for juveniles are the mechanisms by which the Home Office and other government departments – including in relation to youth justice the new Department for Children, Schools and Families that now also shares that responsibility with the Ministry of Justice (MOJ) – are committed 'to:

- supporting or challenging anti-social households;
- tackling truancy and anti-social behaviour in schools;

---

[21] In magistrates' courts the normal summary limit applies, i.e. six months and/or £5,000; rising to 12 months under non-implemented provisions of the Criminal Justice Act 2003.

[22] This partially followed the model of the Protection from Harassment Act 1997; although under those provisions civil and criminal processes run in parallel to each other.

[23] Hence, also, the coining of terms such as 'asbomania'.

[24] One day count of anti-social behaviour: 10 September 2003.

- providing activities for younger people;
- strengthening local communities; and
- stronger measures to tackle anti-social behaviour.'

Hence what was a wholly new device originally intended to be used sparingly and in relation to a few problem families has moved from the margins of crime prevention/crime reduction strategy to the mainstream; and whilst independent organizations such as ASBO Concern[25] exist to monitor, comment on and make representation to the Home Office concerning the risks that are inherent in over use of ASBOs and the fact that they ultimately and inevitably bring more and more people into the 'criminal justice net' for relatively low-level misbehaviour, the ASBO would now appear to be firmly entrenched as one of the most telling developments in crime prevention/crime reduction for many decades.

[25] A consortium of organizations with interests in this field: see www.asboconcern.org.uk

Terrorism and Emergency Powers

CHAPTER 5

Terrorism and Emergency Powers

It is generally recognised in both international and national law[1] that Governments must be free to take special measures to defend and protect their countries and citizens from large scale attacks or similar emergencies whether these are in the nature of war, terrorism or of a purely civil variety. The term 'emergency powers' may be used to describe legislation or other measures that are enacted or relied upon in such circumstances, although in modern times the term 'terrorism legislation' has been to the fore. Naturally, such measures often involve a diminution in individual rights in the broader interests of the entire population and according to what is deemed by ministers to be appropriate and proportionate to the threat.

The UK Government has from time-to-time sought powers to deal with short-term emergencies, e.g. relating to industrial action or vital services, or to prevent picketing and intimidation; usually by presenting a Bill that Parliament has enacted under a special fast-track procedure, with the resulting statute lapsing after a set period unless renewed. Legislation on terrorism took a similar form in the 1970s due to The Troubles in Northern Ireland (below). It may sometimes involve derogation from the European Convention On Human Rights (ECHR) or reliance on national security exemptions. The modern-day global threats from terrorism and the always present possibility of a biological, gas or nuclear attack has led to new anti-terrorist measures of the kind described later in this chapter. In certain circumstances emergency powers can be taken by ministers without first referring to Parliament;[2] when the home secretary is normally to the fore and the Home Office the lead department. These are kept under close review and the home secretary is accountable to Parliament for his or her actions (or in the courts if such actions are challenged as wrong in law which is not uncommon, especially if such legislation impacts too widely). Potentially, new forms of democratic engagement noted *Chapters 1* and *10* suggest that Parliament is likely to be allowed greater input *before* such action is taken.

TERRORISM

In everyday parlance, the words 'terrorism' and 'terrorist' are used to refer, if somewhat elastically, to events or participants in them, respectively, in which

---

[1] Sometimes called domestic law.
[2] See, especially *Confronting Terrorism/COBRA* below.

terror is generated by means of the use of substantial or systematic violence, intimidation and fear but there is no internationally agreed definition. The UK's Terrorism Act 2000 defines terrorism as follows:

1. (1) In this Act 'terrorism' means the use or threat of action where-
   (a) the action falls within subsection (2),
   (b) the use or threat is designed to influence the government or to intimidate the public or a section of the public, and
   (c) the use or threat is made for the purpose of advancing a political, religious or ideological cause.
   (2) Action falls within this subsection if it-
   (a) involves serious violence against a person,
   (b) involves serious damage to property,
   (c) endangers a person's life, other than that of the person committing the action,
   (d) creates a serious risk to the health or safety of the public or a section of the public, or
   (e) is designed seriously to interfere with or seriously to disrupt an electronic system.
   (3) The use or threat of action falling within subsection (2) which involves the use of firearms or explosives is terrorism whether or not subsection (1)(b) is satisfied.
   (4) In this section-
   (a) 'action' includes action outside the United Kingdom,
   (b) a reference to any person or to property is a reference to any person, or to property, wherever situated,
   (c) a reference to the public includes a reference to the public of a country other than the United Kingdom, and
   (d) 'the government' means the government of the United Kingdom, of a Part of the United Kingdom or of a country other than the United Kingdom.
   (5) In this Act a reference to action taken for the purposes of terrorism includes a reference to action taken for the benefit of a proscribed organisation.

As per the 2000 Act above, terrorism is concerned with political, religious or ideological ends rather than, e.g. the proceeds of crime *per se*, although interconnections between organized crime and terrorism cannot be ignored. Terrorists *are* criminal offenders and terrorism may be funded by acquisitive crimes such as robberies, fraud, blackmail (including ransom demands) or money laundering – whilst gangland, the underworld and 'rogue states' in breach if international law and human rights may, e.g. be involved in the supply of weapons and resources. It extends to cyber-terrorism (subsection (2)(e) above). As the 2000 Act also makes clear among other things, jurisdiction is extra-territorial and the law also protects devolved parts of the UK. Taken together with subsequent provisions, the reach of terrorism law is extensive. Various eminent lawyers and commentators have pointed out that it is not possible to interpret the law so that it 'catches' virtually anyone who acts or speaks out in any way against the political status quo.

Home Office statements and announcements regularly emphasise the criminal nature of terrorism.[3] Another general stance is that neither the state, the police, security services or other authorities will 'negotiate' with terrorists in response to their demands,[4] nor can even the most liberal or understanding of Governments realistically acknowledge the oft-heard maxim that one person's terrorist is another's freedom fighter.

Historically, the word 'terrorism' has been applied to a wide range of events, from uprisings and rebellions to other plots and conspiracies against the Crown or state and also to 'activists' of various kinds – including of a quasi-military or paramilitary nature. Terrorism may be used in an attempt to coerce Governments, communities or powerful economic interests to accede to given demands concerning aspects of (often high or widely impacting) policy. Such events may involve the use of bombs, explosives, arson, guns, missiles and other weapons, even the hijacking of aircraft. Perhaps the most notorious attack was that on the The World Trade Center, New York on 11 September 2001 (below).

Twice towards the end of the 20th century there were determined terrorist attempts to assassinate a UK prime minister.[5] Similarly, but of a lesser – and maybe more unpredictable nature – there are the actions of, e.g. a lone terrorist who threatens to poison food in supermarkets or the water supply, or a so-called 'unabomber'. In modern times, UK terrorism has been chiefly associated with The Troubles in Northern Ireland (now largely resolved but with occasional agitation by paramilitary splinter groups) and attacks attributed to al-Qaida; the latter proving to be of particular concern due to the hidden or nebulous nature of the threat to security, religious connotations that can be traced back for many hundreds of years and the ease with which it appears to have been possible to recruit British 'home grown' adherents to jihad (holy war) (see in this chapter).

Terrorism: the general law and dedicated terrorism legislation
Protection against terrorism relies both on the ordinary criminal law but also on any special legislation, frequently termed 'Terrorism Acts' of the kind already quoted from above. Under the general law, e.g. terrorists may be charged with murder, causing explosions, possessing offensive weapons and the like. Since 2000 and in response to new threats of the kind described below the UK has passed a series of terrorism Acts, whilst other provisions may contain special

---

[3]   As, e.g. at www.homeoffice.gov.uk. Such language is also common in Parliament.

[4]   The reality may be different - and with 'high politics' a stage may come, as in Northern Ireland, when open channels for dialogue are essential (see later in the chapter).

[5]   Of Margaret Thatcher in the Brighton Bombing (1984) and a mortar attack on John Major in Downing Street (1991) both by the Irish Republican Army (IRA).

exemptions in the case of terrorism.[6] It would be impossible here to describe the full impact of this legislation but some main strands can be noted, i.e. the:

- Terrorism Act 2000 that continues to be a central focus for counter-terrorism legislation and contains definitions and a number of vital counter-terrorism measures, including, e.g. powers under which over 40 international terrorist organizations have been banned in the sense of being 'proscribed';
- Anti-terrorism, Crime and Security Act 2001 that among other things sought to cut off terrorist funding and allowed the police to target terrorist cash and property and obtain freezing orders; ensured that government departments and agencies can collect and share information required for countering the terrorist threat; streamlined relevant immigration procedures; sought to protect the security of the nuclear and aviation industries and improve the security of dangerous substances that might be targeted or used by terrorists; amended (under the heading 'Weapons of Mass Destruction') the Biological Weapons Act 1974 and the Chemical Weapons Act 1996; extended police

---

[6] Concern has been expressed about the use of the terrorism legislation to deal with 'ordinary law-abiding protesters' – known as 'function creep' - despite Government assurances that this would not happen; and thus, according to the human rights group Liberty, such legislation 'should not be used to curb legitimate protest'. The dilemma can also be gleaned from a letter that appeared in *The Guardian* newspaper (24 November 2001) from an A C Grayling noting that the old Sedition Act and current Official Secrets Act were each passed in times of emergency (the latter as a 'temporary measure' but still extant). He wrote: '. . . it is precisely in times of emergency that a people has to be at its most vigorous in defending its civil liberties, for that is when governments take the opportunity to limit them, preaching necessity'. Notoriously, 'everyday victims' of terror crackdowns include Brian Haw who has been living and demonstrating in Parliament Square since 2001 protesting at UK-USA involvement in the Iraq War and its aftermath and who has effectively defeated attempts to remove him via the courts; Walter Wolfgang, an 80-years-old pensioner, forcibly removed from a hall for heckling the then foreign secretary, Jack Straw (2005); Maya Evans convicted under anti-terrorism legislation after refusing a police instruction to stop reading out loud from a list of dead soldiers at the Cenotaph in Whitehall (2005); Mark Barratt prosecuted for holding an anti-war tea party on Westminster Green; and John Catt, again aged 80 arrested on Brighton, Sussex beach for wearing an 'anti-Tony Blair' t-shirt (2005). The private sector has also been criticised as when the British Airports Authority sought to use the Prevention From Harassment Act 1997 (enacted to deal with stalkers but now widely used to secure civil injunctions, criminal convictions and retraining orders across a broad front) was refused an excessively wide-ranging injunction against a consortium – that included some household name membership organizations - supporting a Camp For Climate Action at Heathrow Airport (2007). For a review of such high profile cases, see *The Independent*, 7 August 2007, 'Joy for protesters as Heathrow is denied "mother of all injunctions"'.

powers available to relevant forces; ensured that the UK could meet European obligations in the area of police and judicial co-operation and international obligations to counter bribery and corruption; and generally updated aspects of the UK's anti-terrorist powers;

- Prevention of Terrorism Act 2005 that introduced control orders to be made against any suspected terrorist, whether a UK national or a non-UK national, or whether the terrorist activity is international or domestic – in replacement for certain powers of detention without trial (below) originally contained in the 2001 Act (above);

- the home secretary is required to report to Parliament as soon as reasonably possible after the end of the relevant three-month period on how control order powers have been exercised during that time, below, amongst other things; and

- the Terrorism Act 2006 that, in particular, created new offences of: committing acts preparatory to terrorism so as to allow the police and security services to move speedily when they believe that an attack is at the planning stage but where the admissible evidence would not necessarily justify an arrest or charge for some substantive offence; glorifying terrorism, a wholly novel offence created in the wake of the London bombings (below) and stemming from a desire by Government to silence extremists and in some instances already forbidden Muslim clerics in particular; inciting terrorism or funding it; or giving or receiving training in the making or handling of explosives; possessing information likely to be of use to terrorists; further provisions in relation to proscribed terrorist organizations.

The Terrorism Act 2000 Act also introduced a power to stop and search people for articles connected to terrorism but without any further or underlying ground for this, in effect to search anyone without giving a reason and at random. By 2007 and following attempted bombings in London and Glasgow this power was being relied on to search some 350 people a day in London alone or almost 11,000 people a month – a five-fold increase on monthly averages before those events. The police indicated that there would be 'no let up'; rather the number of searches would increase.[7] According to one MPS commander:

---

[7] The police have general powers to stop and search on reasonable suspicion (under the so-called 'sus laws'), principally for drugs, weapons and stolen property. Of 10,948 'terrorism stops' in July 2007, the targets were 24% Asian people, 14% black and 54% white (Metropolitan Police Service). The operation of the sus laws has often been criticised for a bias towards searching members of minority groups, seemingly now exacerbated re terrorism searches by the 'Muslim factor' referred to in this chapter. There had previously been a promise to scale back on such searches including following complaints by Muslim leaders concerning victimisation and a risk of alienation.

Terrorists live. Work and blend into our communities. They need accommodation, transport, communications, materials and storage. Terrorists can come from any background and live anywhere. They are as likely to be seen in quiet suburban roads as they are in inner city areas … to complement our more covert methods … we must have a more visible presence to deter and prevent terrorist activity.

Various further measures were included in the Serious and Organized Crime and Police Act 2005 (see, generally, *Chapter 3*) including powers for the police to restrict demonstrations and protest. A further Terrorism Bill is about to be placed before Parliament at the time of writing, the contents of which reflect Government assurances set out in *Appendix II* to this work.

Practical arrangements
The Government also appointed an Anti-Terror Czar and, in 2007, a National Coordinator for Terrorist Investigations, Peter Clarke.[8] There is also an independent reviewer of anti-terrorism legislation, Lord Carlisle and a new Home Office security minister, Lord West. Its broader and more wide-ranging national security strategies and developing arrangements under the Cabinet Intelligence and Security Committee have already been described in *Chapter 2*. The specific fight against terrorism (as it is often styled) relies on various other devices and mechanisms as:

- the creation of modern-day security organizations including the Joint Terrorism Analysis Centre (JTAC) and an Office for Security and Counter-Terrorism (OSCT) and special training in relation to terrorist incidents extending to chemical, biological and nuclear (CBRN) resilience and related decontamination arrangements (all mentioned later in the chapter);
- Home Office direct links to the security services MI5 and GCHQ and partnership with MI6 (all further noted below);
- international co-operation including extensive exchange of information;
- use of the private sector where appropriate although the extent of this is hard to assess given the secrecy of relevant Government contracts;
- the banning of organizations by placing them on a list;[9]
- the closure of premises associated with terrorism;[10]
- detention without trial (below);

---

[8] A deputy assistant commissioner with the MPS (later criticised by the Independent Police Complaints Commission (IPCC) re police communications in the aftermath of the Stockwell Shooting mentioned in the footnotes to *Chapter 3*). The MPS has its own anti-terrorist unit; as do various provincial police forces.

[9] Hence they are known as 'listed organizations'.

[10] Notably for a long period in 2005/6, the Finsbury Park Mosque, North London and later various madrassas (Muslim colleges) suspected of encouraging extremism.

- control orders (below); and
- enhancements in technology of the kind described in *Chapters 3* and *10*.

The security services have also been involved in mock terrorism exercises such as those that have taken place when parts of London have been sealed off from the public for the police, fire, ambulance and other emergency services to rehearse their respective roles. This involved ministers watching from the steps of The Guildhall whilst a simulated sarin poison gas attack was carried out on the London Underground (as earlier occurred in real life in Japan). The exercise was overseen by London Resilience,[11] a body charged with co-ordinating government responses in relation to this variety of attack.

Some facts and figures

The UK police terrorism arrest statistics (excluding Northern Ireland) from 11 September 2001 to 31 March 2007 show that 1228 arrests were made: including 1165 under the Terrorism Act 2000 and 63 under other legislation but where the investigation was conducted as a terrorist investigation. Of the total 1228 arrests:

- 132 people were charged with terrorism legislation offences only;
- 109 were charged with terrorism legislation offences plus other criminal offences;
- 195 were charged under other legislation including murder, grievous bodily harm, firearms, explosives offences, fraud, false documents;
- 76 were handed to the immigration authorities (see, generally, *Chapter 6*)
- 15 people were on police bail awaiting charging decisions;
- one warrant was issued for arrest;
- 12 people were cautioned;
- one was dealt with under youth justice procedures;
- eleven were dealt with under mental health legislation;
- four were transferred to Police Service of Northern Ireland custody;
- two were remanded in custody awaiting extradition proceedings;
- 669 people were released without charge; and
- one case was awaiting further investigation.

Of those charged, there were 41 Terrorism Act convictions; 183 people convicted under other legislation: murder and explosives offences (including conspiracies), grievous bodily harm, firearms offences, fraud, false documents offences, etc (including the 12 cautions already noted above); and 114 awaiting their trial.[12]

---

[11] 'Resilience' is a term used re certain kinds of critical attack: see later in the chapter.

[12] Source: based on figures compiled from police records by the offices of the National Co-ordinator for Terrorist Investigations.

The shifting sands of terrorism

Terrorism is always problematic in terms of its covert, disguised and wholly subversive nature, the existence of parallel worlds (that of the law-abiding citizen and the secret world of self-believing and committed activists), subterfuge and intrigue. But the terrorism of today differs markedly from that of the past in being a global phenomenon within a highly mobile world; and that may involve outright fanatics who, as in the case of al-Qaida, see their own radicalisation or even death in terms of a crusade, their fight and potential martyrdom sanctioned by their religious beliefs. Comparing the UK's experience of al-Qaida with that of The Troubles in Northern Ireland gives some indication of the adjustments that have needed to take place in trying to combat terrorism.

The Troubles in Northern Ireland

In modern times in the UK and from the 1970s onwards terrorism was mostly associated with events in Northern Ireland when paramilitary organizations on both sides of a divide whose origins go back for centuries regularly committed atrocities on each other, on civilian populations or meted out forms of rough justice including punishment beatings. The backdrop includes various iconic allusions to Oliver Cromwell's unwelcome sorties into Ireland in the mid-1600s, William of Orange and the Battle of the Boyne in which the British secured supremacy (1690) and the Easter Rising (1916) following which 14 republican ringleaders were executed by firing squad. Other iconic references over the years include such matters as internment, the H-blocks of The Maze Prison (where prisoners from both sides of the divide were held), hunger strikes in an attempt to gain political prisoner status,[13] The Bogside, historic plantation schemes that deprived Irish landowners and farmers of their heritage, Home Rule and later partition of the country, Croke Park where Gaelic football supporters were gunned down by the Irish Republican Army (IRA), Armagh, Wexford, Land Laws, Penal Laws, the Phoenix Park murders of British government officials, the Manchester Martyrs, several Bloody Sundays, the aggressiveness of the Black and Tans and their quasi-British military approach to policing, the deployment of troops to assist the Royal Ulster Constabulary from the 1979s onwards and alleged 'shoot to kill' policies, later investigated by Lord Stevens a former MPS commissioner, but never wholly resolved.

The full background to all this could never be conveyed in a book of this kind. The central point is that the events had a discernible background against which it was possible to gradually work towards some kind of solution. With hindsight, the transition from The Troubles to a power-sharing devolved Government in Northern Ireland in 2007 following the Good Friday Agreement

---

[13] Including the death in 1981 of Bobby Sands and nine other republican internees.

of 1998 is likely to rank as a considerable achievement as brought about by the New Labour Government led by prime minister Tony Blair.[14] As complex or incomprehensible as events in Northern Ireland were, they permitted of a rational or logical approach.

Al-Qaida

Far less obvious or potentially negotiable[15] are the problems of al-Qaida and associated Muslim extremists, which are also inextricably bound up with politics in the Middle East and wars in Afghanistan and Iraq (the latter officially ended in 2003 and now described as 'a conflict', although large numbers of USA and to a seemingly decreasing extent UK troops still occupy that country as it seeks to govern itself). Terrorism by such extremists began to hit home in the UK with the London suicide bombings of 7 July 2005 mentioned at the start of this book when a series of home made explosive devices were simultaneously placed on the London Underground system and a London Transport bus, killing 52 people. There have since been some 15 failed or aborted attacks,[16] including an attempt to blow up a transatlantic passenger jet in mid-flight in 2006 and a car bomb attack on Glasgow Airport in July 2007. Other notably high profile events include the Ricin Plot to use poison to contaminate public places or water supplies and the shooting dead of John Charles De Menezes at Stockwell Underground station, North London on 22 July 2005 in mistake for one of the July 21 suspects. There have also been various major raids of premises but which have often been abortive, including, e.g. at Forest Gate, North London.

This modern day form of terrorism has also been linked to such threats as the possible use of a dirty bomb (see, generally, under *Resilience*, below). Hence a different approach and the outwardly heavy-handed nature of certain of the terrorism provisions already mentioned earlier in this chapter that have frequently proved highly controversial. Whilst some people argue that fear is generated unnecessarily others perceive a far more insidious threat than has ever existed historically with a faceless enemy[17] that is part of a cultural divide between East and West; and in which security measures risk alienating or marginalising sections of a law-abiding Muslim population. Hence, latterly, political moves to win hearts and minds, concerning ideology, discussions of Britishness and enhanced border controls (see *Chapter 6* and *Appendix III*) and doubts over multi-culturalism. There is a potent mix in which race, religion, hate,

---

[14] But a significant number of commentators link 'the war on terror' with al-Qaida with both the ending of the Cold War and the end of hostilities in Northern Ireland: usually those who argue that the 'politics of fear' have simply shifted to a convenient place.

[15] For it is clear that Governments may ultimately 'negotiate' if high policy is involved.

[16] Announcement by prime minister Gordon Brown (July 2007).

[17] Albeit that much is attributed to the, until now, elusive Osama Bin Laden.

fanaticism, fear and xenophobia intertwine. Hence, e.g. wide-ranging and international shifts of emphasis such as those propounded by prime minister Gordon Brown to American President George Bush concerning the need to engage in a cultural, intellectual and counter-insurgency programme of the kind that was used to counter the communism of the Union of Soviet Socialist Republics during the Cold War.[18]

Confronting terrorism

The day-to-day mechanisms for dealing with terrorism and other emergencies are wide-ranging. They exist as a backdrop to everyday policing and alertness as well as within special operations. Centrally, the Home Office discharges its responsibilities via a number of standing arrangements.

COBRA

Cobra is the somewhat colourful name for the civil contingencies committee which leads responses to national crises, including major threats to public security such as terrorism. The group, named after Cabinet Office Briefing Room A (in the bowels of Downing Street) where it normally holds its meetings,[19] was convened in recent times following September 11, July 7, July 21 and the Glasgow Airport attack of 2007 (see earlier in this chapter), but also for a range of events from international incidents through fuel protests to outbreaks of bird-flu or foot and mouth disease in animals. The membership of COBRA varies according to the issue under consideration, and can often include the prime minister, home secretary or other senior ministers (who usually chair matters) and police, security and intelligence chiefs – and officials and representatives of affected departments at the highest level. The seniority of COBRA's membership ensures that it quickly establishes what needs to be done and that action is taken rapidly, mobilising resources, personnel and facilities as appropriate.

It also considers items such as whether to invoke emergency powers such as those contained in civil contingencies legislation, e.g. in the event of a chemical, radiological or biological attack or a 'dirty bomb'. These powers, often ultimately falling to the prime minister or home secretary as appropriate, can allow him or her, e.g. to suspend Parliament and to temporarily close down businesses, in effect to impose a 'security holiday'. Similarly in such circumstances and by executive decree, property can be destroyed or requisitioned, assemblies can be banned and freedom of movement or association can be ended or restricted. Ultimately, in the face of a major atrocity or threat, the armed forces can be mobilised and martial law declared to deal with suspects via special courts. Theoretically people can be forced to comply with instructions or policies by

---

[18] See, particularly, an article by Matthew d'Ancona in *The Spectator*, 2 August 2007.
[19] Meetings of COBRA may also be held at other places in Whitehall.

whatever means and due to the nature of events and the terms of the Human Rights Act 1998 regard to human rights.

The New Security and Counter-Terrorism Science and Innovation Strategy
A new Home Office strategy (2007) gives details of how the department intends to work with its partners in the private sector and academia, international colleagues, and within Government, 'to use science and innovation' so as to strengthen the UK's counter-terrorism capabilities. Four specific ways are identified by which the Home Office will seek to achieve this, i.e. by:

- expanding a cross-departmental approach to identifying Government's counter-terrorism research priorities;
- horizon-scanning for future threats and new scientific developments to counter such threats;
- working more effectively with business and academia to ensure research is delivered and exploited through the cultivation of a strong and innovative counter-terrorism research market; and
- collaboration with international partners, allowing increased sharing of knowledge and technologies.

Contemporaneous announcements included:

- a national security strategy to be published in autumn 2007;
- a single security budget starting at the next spending review;
- the chair of the Joint Intelligence Committee would be independent;
- the Government would consult on how the members of the Intelligence and Security Committee should be appointed, and on how it should report to Parliament; and
- there would be electronic screening of all passengers travelling into and from the UK.

According to prime minister Gordon Brown when announcing the NSC, the first line of defence against terrorism is overseas where people initially embark on their journeys to the UK, bringing about a need to accelerate plans to replace outmoded and ineffective paper-based systems and replacement them with 'real-time monitoring', that would allow for immediate action and full co-ordination across immigration, police and intelligence (see, also, generally, *Chapters 3* and *8*):

> The way forward is electronic screening of all passengers as they check in and out of our country at ports and airports - so that terrorist suspects can be identified and stopped before they board planes, trains and boats to the United Kingdom.

Hence a need to enhance the existing e-Borders programme (*Chapter 6*).

Office for Security and Counter-Terrorism (OSCT)

This provides advice to ministers, develops policy and provides security measures to combat the threat of terrorism. The OSCT has led the work on counter-terrorism in the UK for over 30 years working closely with the police (*Chapter 3*) and security services (below). The attacks in the USA on 11 September 2001 altered the way that OSCT functions. The number of partners and stakeholders was expanded to draw in all the emergency services; local and regional government; and even closer working with international partners. Since that time, the Home Office has also sought to make more information publicly accessible without undermining national security. The OSCT reports to the home secretary and minister of state at the Home Office. It has responsibility for:

- exercising the UK's response to a terrorist incident;
- developing legislation relating to terrorism in the United Kingdom and overseas;
- providing appropriate protective security measures and protection packages for public figures at risk;
- ensuring that the UK's critical national infrastructure is protected from attack (including electronic attack);
- ensuring the UK is prepared to deal with a chemical, biological, or nuclear release; and
- liaising between government and the emergency services during terrorist incidents or counter-terrorism operations.

The OSCT also oversees the administration of the Regulation of Investigatory Powers Act 2000 (RIPA); Security Service Acts 1989 and 1996; and Home Office aspects of Intelligence Services Act 1994.

Chemical, biological, radiological and nuclear (CBRN) resilience

The CBRN resilience programme brings together expertise on chemical, biological, radiological and nuclear terrorism from across government and partner agencies. It is led by the Home Office and was established as part of the Government's Capability Programme in 2001, with the main aim of ensuring that, in the event of a terrorist incident the response from all concerned will be quick and effective, with the result that lives are saved, and the impact on property and the environment is minimised. Since the resilience programme was established much progress has been made in increasing the UK's capability to respond to a CBRN incident, including:

- better personnel training;
- improved detection and decontamination equipment; and
- more effective personal protective equipment (PPE).

The two bodies running the CBRN Resilience Programme are the CBRN Strategic Board and the CBRN Performance and Delivery Group. The board is made up of senior representatives from all the key delivery partners, and is chaired by the Home Office. It is responsible for the programme policy, direction and prioritisation. The Performance and Delivery Group reports to the Strategic Board and is also chaired by the Home Office. Made up of representatives from all the main delivery partners it is responsible for generating proposals for new work as well as monitoring programme performance. Other supporting groups chaired by the Home Office include a:

- Tacticians Forum;
- CBRN Partners Forum; and
- CBRN Science and Technology Programme.

Decontamination
In some circumstances a release of CBRN materials may mean those affected and the environment may need to be decontaminated. Decontamination might not always be necessary but would be used as a precaution depending on circumstances and the judgment of those in charge on the ground. During an incident trained medical staff and members of the emergency services would assess and advise the public, recording their details before allowing them home. Assessment on what may be required for the environment or buildings would take place over a longer period of time. The priority is public safety.

Policy responsibilities for decontamination issues are shared between government departments: the Department of Health, the Department for the Environment, Food and Rural Affairs (Defra), the Department for Communities and Local Government (DCLG, formerly the Office of the Deputy Prime Minister), and the Home Office. Under the CBRN resilience programme a suite of decontamination guidance has been developed on population management and decontamination following an incident (the latter resting with the Department of Health). According to the nature of land and buildings decontamination, lead responsibility rests with Defra or the DCLG.

The Home Office and its partners across government ensure that the emergency services have the best and most appropriate equipment and training available to respond to CBRN incidents. Much of the equipment and training is the same as would be used during accidental hazardous materials (HAZMAT) incidents although with dedicated procedures. Additional investment made to counter the effects of CBRN has also strengthened the emergency services response to HAZMAT incidents.[20] In order to develop essential expertise in dealing with a CBRN incident, training is provided for emergency service personnel at the Police National CBRN Centre and the Fire Service College. Training and guidance for government staff and public service staff is provided by an Emergency Planning College.

The Police National CBRN Centre (PN-CBRN-C)

The Police National CBRN Centre was established in October 2001 on the Winterbourne Gunner site of the Ministry of Defence (MOD) which is situated on Salisbury Plain. This centre of excellence provides high quality training and support to the Home Office and the police concerning responses to CBRN incidents. As early as 2005, some 7,000 UK police officers had been trained and equipped to deal with a CBRN incident, the majority by dedicated PN-CBRN-C specialists. One purpose is to ensure officers have the necessary skills and equipment to respond effectively to CBRN incidents and to provide:

- strategy and training service;
- research and development advice, including best practice and procedures in relation to operational issues; and
- an emergency equipment procurement process.

The centre concentrates on developing the personal skills, abilities and qualities of its staff and students and on providing advice and guidance on all police CBRN issues and related operational matters, including identifying, collating and disseminating information and best practice. Its work also involves developing doctrine, protocols and procedures in relation to police operational responses to a CBRN incident.

---

[20] Thus, e.g. every acute hospital and ambulance service has been equipped with standardised personal protective equipment (PPE). Some 7,250 personal protection suits have been distributed to key health workers and a further 2,500 of these suits stockpiled. Some 4,400 gas tight suits – a doubling of former capacity – have been purchased for the fire service so that fire-fighters can decontaminate safely and so as to allow them to take part in rescues. Bespoke personal protective equipment (CR1 suits) has been provided for the police service. All three emergency services have officers equipped and trained in the use of PPE that allows them to attend an incident where there has been a release of CBRN material. The CR1 suit is currently being rolled out to all CBRN trained police officers. The police previously used military-style suits.

A unified border force

In July 2007, Gordon Brown, prime minister reported to Parliament his assessment of the UK terrorism threat, when he also announced that the existing Border and Immigration Agency, Customs and UK Visas, would in future operate overseas and at the main points of entry into the UK as a unified border force (see *Chapter 6*). At that time and indicative of the nature of modern-day Government support and pronouncements on terrorism, he praised those involved in foiling recent terrorist attacks in London and Glasgow (the 15th attempted terrorism attack on British soil since 2001, he noted), saying that:

> Britain, led by London and Glasgow, stood firm in the face of threats, and our calmness and steadfastness sent a powerful message across the world that we will not yield to terrorism, nor ever be intimidated by it . . . the police and security services currently battle 30 known plots, while monitoring more than 200 groups and in excess of 2,000 suspected terrorists ... [All countries now face a] generation-long challenge to defeat al-Qaida-inspired violence.

THE SECURITY SERVICES: A NOTE

Security has become a complex business in the modern world that involves both the state and private sectors and at various levels of responsibility. At the highest level and in terms of 'homeland security'[21] the Home Office relies both on everyday policing (and its extensions such as Special Branch[22] and now the Serious and Organized Crime Agency (SOCA)) (*Chapter 3*) part of whose role is to 'harry, hassle and hound' terrorists and organized criminals, the home branch of the security service, MI5, and the government listening station GCHQ (below). Both these latter agencies come within the broader remit of the Home Office. However, the foreign secretary and his or her Foreign and Commonwealth Office retain responsibility with regards to MI6, sometimes described as 'the external security service'.[23] But all must work together and in partnership, not least due to the international flavour of everyday affairs that now exists within any nation state and there are countless aspects of security, public safety and law enforcement in which, e.g. the interests and intelligence demands of the police, border agency, MI5, MI6 and defence services coincide or overlap.

---

[21] This Americanism seems to have arrived in the UK some time in the early 2000s.

[22] The term 'Special Branch' may now be a misnomer since such activities have mainly been incorporated into the work of SOCA: but it seems that local police forces may retain their own 'special branch' and the term is still regularly used in the media.

[23] Notwithstanding that at the time of the Home Office split, the then home secretary, Dr John Reid, sought to have that responsibility transferred to himself: *Chapter 1*.

To take a live and current example, Foreign Office moves to persuade the USA authorities to return British residents held as suspected terrorists at Guantánamo Bay, the USA's special Cuban offshore detention centre, have obvious implications for the Home Office in terms of subsequent home policing, monitoring, surveillance and information in relation to such suspects. Similarly, extraordinary rendition flights whereby suspects have been transported by the American CIA to a country where human rights are less well-protected than in the USA or the European Union - and that land at UK airports en route - automatically trigger a Home Office interest. In practice, much nowadays rests on the work of the Joint Intelligence Committee (JIC) (below) and its various components and networks.

MI5

As already indicated, MI5 operates under the statutory aegis of the home secretary but it is not part of the Home Office as such. As the home branch of the Secret Intelligence Service (SIS) - originally styled Department 5 of the then new Directorate of Military Intelligence (DMI) (hence MI5) formed in 1916 as a development of the 'old Secret Intelligence Service' (1909 onwards) and Secret Service Bureau (SSB) (late-1800s) - MI5 later evolved, from the 1930s onwards, via an amalgamation with a Special Section of Scotland Yard involved in covert policing and also in partnership with the ordinary civil police.

With the Home Secretary, the agency takes responsibility for such key public safety matters as the protection of the UK from threats to its national security, terrorism, sabotage and work by agents of foreign states within the UK; as well as threats from whatever source that might tend towards the overthrow or undermining of the status quo of democracy – whether by violent, political,[24] industrial, criminal or other means. In accordance with the Security Service Act 1989, it also gives advice on security to a range of organizations from the public sector and private sector; carries out work to counter the proliferation of weapons; and assists broadly by lending support to crime prevention and crime reduction strategies (*Chapter 4*). The extent to which it works directly alongside the police depends on day-to-day security considerations and demands.

---

[24] The idea of agents of the state disrupting political threats may seem odd in a democracy where the ballot box should determine such matters: but this is not one for theoretical purists it seems, so that an element of imagination is needed in which, for democracy to survive at all, it was at some stage assumed and then became entrenched that the UK must be protected from any extreme power bases of whatever political hue. Hence, e.g. the now revealed efforts of MI5 to undermine communism from the 1950s onwards, or covert policing of fascists, the National Front or British National Party (BNP).

MI5 is headed by a director-general (D-G) and has various branches. As with the other security agencies, it is funded via the Single Intelligence Account (SIA); and like them it operates to gather, analyse and optimise the use of relevant data and information; including under the auspices of National Intelligence Machinery (NIM) as co-ordinated by the Joint Intelligence Committee (JIC) (below). In modern times, there has been a strong emphasis on recruitment across a broader section of the population than hitherto (when appointment was associated with 'Old Boy Networks'), including especially of people with special skills, from minority communities or with a close knowledge, e.g. of languages and cultural or religious imperatives.[25]

MI6

MI6 operates under the aegis of the Foreign Secretary and Foreign Office as the foreign branch of the SIS. It was originally styled Department 6 of the Directorate of Military Intelligence (DMI)(1916) (and hence MI6).[26] It has responsibility, in particular, for gathering intelligence from abroad in support of security, defence and foreign and economic policy considerations within a framework of requirements laid down by the JIC (below) and subsequently approved by ministers. It uses a range of sources: human, electronic and technology-based – as well as liaison with co-operative foreign security services worldwide. Major operations are subject to longstanding procedures for official and ministerial clearance in advance; but may also be authorised retrospectively in an unavoidable emergency. MI6 is based at Vauxhall Cross, London. In an intriguing insight, the extent to which the UK relies on Saudi Arabia for intelligence about terrorism and the Middle-East in general was revealed in 2007 by the decision of the UK attorney-general, Lord Goldsmith, to halt a longstanding investigation into bribery at BAE systems in relation to defence contracts with Saudi interests. So great, it seems, were the implications for UK national security of continuing a major criminal investigation that might have fractured international relationships that the investigation was stopped.[27]

Government Communications Headquarters (GCHQ)

GCHQ based in Cheltenham, Gloucestershire is the government 'listening station'. It is concerned with such matters as the interception of communications, code breaking and interpretation. A contentious law enforcement issue of modern times has been whether 'intercept evidence' should become admissible

---

[25] This being one of the triggers for a review of the role of the attorney general as further described in the companion volume to this work, *The New Ministry of Justice*.

[26] A more detailed look reveals that MI6 evolved gradually from 1909-1916 and that it only finally emerged as a wholly separate service within SIS by 1920.

[27] MI6 is based at Thames House, Westminster.

in court. Since taking over as prime minister, Gordon Brown has announced to Parliament that a review would consider, amongst other things, whether to allow intercept evidence, i.e. that from covert surveillance operations generally but specifically involving interception of communications as practised by GCHQ. Such evidence is not currently used as a matter of practice by UK prosecutors largely due to concerns expressed by the security services that this could expose its working methods, reveal sources and put agents or informants at risk.[28]

The Joint Intelligence Committee (JIC)
The JIC is part of the Cabinet Office and is responsible for providing ministers senior departmental officials and others with co-ordinated interdepartmental intelligence assessments on a range of issues of immediate and long-term significance to the national interest, primarily in the fields of security, defence and foreign affairs. The JIC also periodically scrutinises the performance of the agencies in achieving collective goals. It comprises senior officials in the Foreign Office, Ministry of Defence (including the head of Defence Intelligence), Home Office, Department of Trade and Industry, Department for International Development, Treasury and Cabinet Office, the heads of MI5, MI6 and GCHQ (above) and of the JIC assessments staff, with other agencies attending and taking part as and when necessary.

An Intelligence, Security and Resilience permanent secretary with direct access to the prime minister chairs the JIC. He or she is responsible for supervising the work of the JIC and is charged specifically with ensuring that the committee's warning and monitoring role is discharged effectively. The JIC is supported by assessment staff: practitioners seconded from a range of related departments, services and working or analytical disciplines. They work closely with the responsible agencies and departments to uncover and assess the extent of risks, in interpreting intelligence, information and data, and so as to report to the JIC. Draft assessments are subject to interdepartmental scrutiny via what are known as Current Intelligence Groups (CIGs) bringing together experts from across-the-range. The JIC agrees most assessments before they go to ministers and senior officials, but, e.g. urgent updates on a fast-developing situation can be issued under the authority of the head of assessment staff. He or she also has an advisory role and is responsible for oversight of a programme of strategic assessments across government.

A professional head of Intelligence Analysis was established within the Cabinet Office in 2005.[29] His or her main tasks are to advise in the security, defence and foreign affairs fields on gaps and duplication in analyst training, on

---

[28] Such evidence is allowed in criminal proceedings in many other jurisdictions.
[29] In part as a Government response to Lord Butler's report on his *Review of Intelligence on Weapons of Mass Destruction* (2004), HC 898.

recruitment of analysts, career structures and interchange opportunities. A priority is the further development of analytic methodology and training for all analysts working in these fields. As with MI5, MI6, CCHQ and the Defence Intelligence Staff (DIS), assessment staff maintain their own contacts and intelligence networks. Liaison arrangements allow access to information and analysis not otherwise available. In the case of countries with which the UK has military alliances or faces a common threat, information is shared so that decisions can be taken on the basis of a common perception.

Joint Terrorism Analysis Centre (JTAC)

JTAC was established in 2003 as part of the development of co-ordinated arrangements for handling and disseminating intelligence in response to the international terrorist threat. It is a multi-agency unit, staffed by members of the security agencies, Defence Intelligence Staff (DIS) and representatives from other relevant departments including the Foreign Office and Home Office, and from the police. Since 2003 it has become widely recognised as an authoritative and effective mechanism for analysing all-source intelligence on the activities, intentions and capabilities of international terrorists who may threaten UK and allied interests at home and worldwide. It sets threat levels and issues timely threat warnings as well as providing more in-depth reports on trends, terrorist networks and their capabilities. The head of JTAC is accountable directly to the director-general of MI5 or MI6 as applicable, who in turn reports to the JIC on JTAC's performance. An 'Oversight Board', chaired by the Cabinet Office, ensures that JTAC meets customer requirements.[30]

Special Branch

Special Branch was originally established within the Metropolitan Police Service in 1833 to deal with broader threats to public order, espionage, sabotage, subversive activities, aspects of immigration, personal protection of individuals, etc. and in particular to combat the activities of the Irish Fenian Brotherhood, but it extended its activities from 1967 onwards to deal with such perceived threats to social disorder, mass protests and large scale demonstrations. Provincial police forces also developed their own special branches. By 2005, Special Branch officers nationwide had doubled to around 4,200 over the previous 25 years and despite the end of the Cold War, the ceasefire in Northern Ireland and the transfer of many responsibilities to the security services. Paid civilians were also employed as agents to provide information and intelligence - sometimes people opposed to the interests they were spying on or vulnerable to coercion due, e.g. to their known criminal associations. Special Branch tasks also included the infiltration of

---

[30] For further information about the JIC and JTAC visit www.intelligence.gov.uk

criminal networks, surveillance and, as with SIS, undermining and disrupting targeted activities. There were comparable and often covert duties in relation to organized crime, particularly where this involved drugs, firearms and people trafficking. In 2002, a BBC television programme, *True Spies*, pointed to the wide extent of Special Branch activities in relation to the Campaign for Nuclear Disarmament (CND) and the Miners Strike of 1984. Special Branch should be contrasted with the security services MI5 and MI6 (above), although it may often have worked with those agencies, particularly so as to carry out the more visible aspects of an operation. After 1992, the former Special Branch role in combatting Irish terrorism was transferred to the security services, and much of its remaining work directed towards other forms of terrorism and the need to monitor people who abuse democratic liberties or are socially disruptive.

Serious and Organized Crime Agency (SOCA)

The work and role of SOCA in disrupting and inhibiting the activities of organized crime and its role as a nationwide agency encompassing many of the former functions of Special Branch is examined in *Chapter 3*. SOCA is equally involved in disrupting terrorist activity by parallel means, including, in particular via intelligence, arrests and targeting the proceeds of crime for seizure.

ARREST, DETENTION AND CONTROL ORDERS

One particular aspect of the criminal justice process that has caused problems in relation to terrorism is that relating to the arrest and detention of a suspect. Under English law and pending charge, the right to hold someone under arrest who is suspected of a criminal offence and thus in detention is governed by the Police and Criminal Evidence Act 1984 (PACE). Under PACE the usual limit is 24 hours unless up to 36 hours is authorised by a senior police office or a warrant of further detention is granted by a court. The upper limit for what is defined as a serious arrestable offence is then 96 hours. After this, the suspect must be charged with an offence or released. Once charged, the Bail Act 1976 comes into operation when either a police officer or a court may grant bail, i.e. authorise the release of the person charged subject to a duty to surrender to bail at some future time for the allegation to be heard, or a court can (or in some very serious situations must) refuse bail within the terms of the 1976 Act. Significantly and a further consideration in this process, once a suspect is charged he or she cannot be further questioned by the police or other investigating officer. Before charge and, if he or she has been detained, whilst the PACE Act clock is still running, questions can be put to the suspect provided that this is in accordance with the PACE Act Codes of Practice that were originally introduced following a number of miscarriages of justice stemming from aggressive questioning techniques.

Police also use the 'window' provided by PACE to secure enough evidence to justify the Crown Prosecution Service (CPS) to authorise the charging of the person who has been detained.

Detention without trial

All these considerations come into play where the investigation is complex. However, special rules were devised in relation to detention without charge vis-à-vis terrorism whereby the suspect could be held, initially, for up to seven days without charge on the authority of a justice of the peace and thereafter for up to 28 days. However, an authorisation by the home secretary for the extended detention without charge of terrorist suspects was held to be unlawful by the UK courts after the case reached the House of Lords.[31] Subsequently, Parliament passed a law allowing detention in terrorist cases for up to 28 days (subject to judicial supervision). A Government move to allow detention for up to 90 days was defeated in the House of Commons.[32] In July 2007, prime minister Gordon Brown announced that the Government wanted to consult widely on the sensitive issues of pre-charge detention, to revisit consideration of the upper limit, and also on post-charge questioning:

> In terrorism court cases in recent years, police and investigators have had to wade through masses of information in relatively limited amounts of time. In one case police had hundreds of mobile phones and computers to investigate, as well as thousands of gigabytes of data, more than 70 locations to search, and thousands of documents on multiple continents. In recent years six people had to be held for 27-28 days while the investigation was underway.

Because of this, he said, 'It is right to explore whether a consensus can be built on the most measured way to deal with this remaining risk'. Subsequent findings by a Parliamentary Select Committee suggest that there is no such consensus.

The Anti-Terrorism, Crime and Security Act 2001 also allowed arrest and charge 'on reasonable suspicion', e.g. of involvement with or links to terrorism on the order of the home secretary. In 2003, the House of Lords ruled, in the case of 13 suspected international terrorists (all foreign nationals) who had been detained under the 2002 Act, that there should be a full hearing concerning the legality of their detention and the Act's compatibility or otherwise with the ECHR and, in particular, Article 5 (the right to liberty and security/no detention

---

[31] Leading to the introduction of control orders and other attempts to circumvent this.

[32] The first Government defeat in the House of Commons since New Labour came to power in 1997. The Government has been defeated several times in the House of Lords during that time. Prime minister Tony Blair had argued in Parliament that the 90 day limit was essential to allow the gathering of evidence and that 'the police have asked for these powers'. Any formal police request has since been denied.

without trial); the UK having then derogated out of Article 5 in this context on grounds of national security.

Control orders

A replacement system of control orders was introduced by the Prevention of Terrorism Act 2005. This allows for such orders to be made against any suspected terrorist, whether he or she is a UK national or a non-UK national, be the terrorism in question global or national. Control orders allow the authorities to impose conditions upon individual suspects, ranging from prohibitions on access to specific items or services (including, e.g. to prevent them using the Internet); as well as preventing association with specified individuals, to those on their movements, or to require him or her to observe a curfew. These conditions are tailored to each case 'to ensure effective disruption and prevention of terrorist activity'.[33]

The home secretary must normally apply to the courts to impose a control order based on an assessment of intelligence information. When the order is made it is automatically referred to the High Court for judicial review. In emergency cases he or she may impose a provisional order which must then be reviewed by the court within seven days. A court may consider the case in open or closed session – depending on the nature and sensitivity of the information in question. Special advocates who have been security vetted are used to represent the interests of suspects in closed sessions. The orders are time limited and may be imposed for a period of up to 12 months at a time; but are then subject to possible renewal on application to the court.

Breach of an obligation imposed by a control order without reasonable excuse is a criminal offence punishable with imprisonment for up to five years and/or an unlimited fine. Individuals who are subject to control order provisions have the option of applying for an anonymity order.

To date the Government has not sought to make a control order requiring derogation from Article 5 of the European Convention On Human Rights (the right to liberty and security). Amongst the leading cases, the High Court has ruled that anti-terrorism control orders made against six men break European human rights laws when Mr Justice Sullivan decided to quash six control orders

---

[33] The Home Office is careful to point out at its web-site that control orders do not mean 'house arrest'. However, Lord Lloyd, a former law lord, told a terrorism conference in June 2007 that in his view control orders were little less than this and without the safeguards of the criminal process. House arrest as such does not exist under the general law of the UK, but it seems to have been achieved (by unclear means) in 1998 in the case of former head of state General Pinochet, pending his extradition.

under Article 5 based on the severity of the restrictions imposed on the six men.[34] In effect, Article 5 prohibits indefinite detention without trial and, although the men were not behind bars, their freedom was severely circumscribed. Little information about them has been disclosed but it appears that all were required to leave their homes and live in Home Office-approved accommodation. They were not allowed to leave those premises for 18 hours per day, they were fitted with electronic tags, and were unable to communicate with anyone without specific Home Office permission.

When control orders were being framed, the government had a choice - to try to work within the limits of the ECHR or derogate from Article 5. Home Office lawyers believed that the orders, draconian as they are, were proportionate and did not require derogation, which explains why Home Secretary John Reid plans to appeal. Lord Carlisle, the independent reviewer of anti-terrorism legislation (see earlier in this chapter), also argues that derogation is not necessary and has stated that he believed adjustments could be made so as to bring these processes within Article 5.

In April, Mr Justice Sullivan ruled that a control order also breached Article 6 of the ECHR (the right to a fair trial). This ruling, too, is being appealed by the government. The Government argues that the requirement to put evidence before a court, even if it is in a closed session and the suspect is not permitted to see it, conforms to Article 6 obligations. But should the Government fail in its two appeals, it would seem to have little choice but to derogate from the convention if it is determined to keep control orders.

As of mid-2007, e.g. it was reported to Parliament by the home secretary that there were 14 control orders in existence; five against British citizens. The home secretary must submit such reports at regular intervals.

---

[34] Indicative of tensions between the Government and judiciary. Some politicians and commentators appear to view such events as proof positive that the ECHR is the nub of the problem – as well as sections of the general population led, e.g. by the *Sun* newspaper that has campaigned for the repeal of the Human Rights Act 1998.

Border Controls, Immigration and Asylum

CHAPTER 6

Border Controls, Immigration and Asylum

It may be a fair assessment to say that, for many years, Home Office responsibilities for controlling the UK border operated in the shadow of more high profile or media-responsive aspects of its work such as policing and (until May 2007) prisons, but since the Home Office split its border controls have been thrown into greater relief. There have been modern-day public concerns about immigration ever since the *Empire Windrush* first docked at Tilbury, London in 1948 bringing Commonwealth citizens, entitled to freely enter the UK without any quotas or other restrictions, from Jamaica in search of work and to settle in the UK.[1] But whilst crime, punishment and terrorism may have grabbed most of the media headlines concern about strangers, anxiety re the unknown and watchfulness in relation to foreigners feature across the annals of both criminal justice and border controls.[2] Similarly, there is a general overlap between those Home Office responsibilities discussed elsewhere in this book and its border responsibilities, not least in modern times, e.g. in relation to drugs, smuggling, organized crime and trafficking of various kinds. The context for border controls thus touches unavoidably on the Home Office's primary responsibilities in relation to public safety and law and order.

CONTROLLING THE UK'S BORDER[3]

As with questions of national security (*Chapters 2* and *5*), border control policy is dealt with centrally at Westminster and not by the devolved governments of Scotland, Wales or Northern Ireland. This chapter looks at four main strands of border control that are geared to the balanced task of excluding individuals who might in some way harm the UK and its people whilst ensuring that, e.g.

---

[1] It having been mistakenly assumed by government, so a common explanation goes, that in opening up the UK border no one would actually want to leave their foreign home.

[2] In the 15th century heretics of various kinds; in the 18th fear of infiltration and an English-style French Revolution; in the early 20th, Russian and German 'strangers' leading to the creation of the security services described in *Chapter 5*. This might be viewed as the counterpart to outlawry of UK offenders in former times or a propensity for forms of social exclusion re offenders or marginal groups of people in modern times.

[3] The modern fashion appears to be to talk of a single UK border albeit abutting on air and sea and involving separate islands; save, that is for e-Borders!

legitimate tourists, business people, professionals or other workers who may be vital to the UK economy are not deterred:

- **immigration**:[4] the entry into the UK of people to live and work here where they entitled to do so or are otherwise allowed permanently into UK;
- **asylum**: the situation in which aliens ask for refuge from their own state (or in some instances from a third party government);
- **deportation**: the process by which aliens are returned to their own country or a third country, including would be visitors who are refused leave to remain in the UK, or those in breach of their visas, notably 'over stayers';
- **extradition**: a system for the transfer of people between participating states under reciprocal treaties or similar agreements, whereby suspects and other fugitives are handed over to law enforcement officers of the requesting state, usually where it is seeking to place them on trial or capture or recapture those fleeing from justice.[5]

E-borders

Each of these functions underpins the UK's rationale for modern-day electronic borders, or e-Borders. The e-Borders programme will ultimately involve advance passenger information about everyone entering or leaving the UK. Biometric visas[6] are already in place for visitors from 'high-risk countries'; and by the spring of 2008 they will have been extended to everyone entering the UK on a visa. From 2009 there will be a new and enhanced system of electronic exit control, whereby passports will be checked against compulsory advance flight passenger lists and databases of known or suspected terrorists; failing which airlines and ferry operators will incur (criminal) 'carrier's liability'. The Home Office is working to enhance cooperation with the border agencies and police of other states, including via joining up databases of suspects and criminal records across the European Union and as between the UK and USA, in particular. Already, the latter has introduced stringent requirements for people travelling to that country, enhanced visa requirements, and extra demands to carriers for electronic data.[7] The UK and USA have also targeted 'travellers of interest', people thought to be using false documents and identities, and other suspects.

The e-Borders programme was created at a cost of some £1.2 billion so as to lead to a modern intelligence-led border control and security framework. The programme also collects information on when people arrive in the UK and when

---

4 Sometimes and perhaps more properly called 'migration'.
5 Including people who may have been tried and sentenced in their absence.
6 See, generally, the comments on science and technology in *Chapters 3* and *8*.
7 Much of it provided by the private sector and dubbed 'lifestyle data'. This has led to 'Big Brother' criticisms, due to the extent to which it may be being accessed.

or whether they leave as they should. It is claimed that as a result of this *bona fide* travellers will gain from faster clearance at points of entry and exit. Passenger numbers are expected to rise to 305 million a year by 201; and it is anticipated by the Home Office that 50 per cent of passengers will be logged by e-Borders by 2009 and 95 per cent by 2011, with special fast track schemes such as Project Iris (below) for regular - in effect security cleared - travellers.

Project Semaphore

The e-Borders programme was initially rolled out as Project Semaphore and runs until mid-2008 until superseded by the full e-Borders system. Project Semaphore captures passenger information on ten routes to the UK (inbound and outbound) selected by multi-agency consensus covering 10 million passengers and matching names against 'watchlists' (below) from UKIS, the police and Revenue and Customs, risk-assessment profiles, and it alerts government agencies. Pending any reorganization a Joint Border Operations Centre (JBOC) is staffed by representatives of the police, customs, the Immigration Service and UK Visas. This 'single window' for carriers enables them to deliver data to Government agencies once only rather than separately to each agency.

Project IRIS

As part of the e-Borders programme (above), Project IRIS (Iris Recognition Immigration System) is being introduced to provide fast and secure automated clearance through the UK immigration control for certain categories of regular travellers using biometric technology. IRIS will store and verify the iris patterns of qualifying travellers, giving watertight confirmation of their identity when they arrive in the UK. IRIS began at Heathrow Airport in 2005 and was later extended to Gatwick, Birmingham, Manchester and Stansted Airports. Within five years, over one million people will be on this system.

The UK's unified border force

In 2007 the Home Office announced a new unified border force and associated measures. Gordon Brown, prime minister, told Parliament[8] that Britain would create such a force that would be operative 'within months', and whose officials would wear a distinctive, common uniform, so as to 'strengthen the powers and surveillance capabilities of those working to stop terrorists and other would-be illegal entrants coming to the UK. That force will integrate the work of the existing BIA (see later in this chapter) with customs officers (part of Revenue and Customs) and UK Visas, the agency that considers applications from people who wish to enter the UK, e.g. to study or conduct international trade. The new

---

[8]   25 July 2007, as part of a wide-ranging report to Parliament on anti-terrorism measures.

agency will operate both overseas and at the main points of entry to the UK. The aims of the existing BIA are noted towards the end of this chapter.

The Identity and Passport Service (IPS)

Passports are a central instrument of international travel to which increasingly sophisticated mechanisms are being developed worldwide as more and more people become increasingly and globally mobile. The IPS was established as an executive agency of the Home Office in 2006 in order to build on the foundations of the UK Passport Service (UKPS) to provide passport services. In conjunction with an embryonic National Identity Scheme (NIS) it now looks to the development of biometric passports and identity cards for British citizens and Irish nationals who are resident in the UK (see, further *Chapter 7*) as a way to ensuring effective border controls in the future. Foreign nationals who are resident in the UK will be included in the NIS by linking that scheme to biometric immigration documents mentioned in an earlier section.

Associated developments include the removal, from June 2007 of the one week, fast track service for first time passport applications by people over the age of 16. This stems from the introduction of face-to-face interviews for all such applicants as part of that process, which now takes up to six weeks.[9]

Inherent powers of the home secretary

Over and above the powers noted in the remainder of this chapter it should be emphasised that the home secretary has certain inherent powers to exclude undesirable aliens, people who are 'not conducive to the public good'.[10] These have been used to exclude aliens in war-time or people involved in organized crime, members of the Mafia, Chinese Triads, Jamaican Yardies and suspected al-Qaida terrorists. In 2006, the then home secretary, Dr John Reid announced that he would use it to exclude foreigners who were involved in the promulgation of extremist views, including 'preachers of hate' who were not welcome in the UK, even if no other law pointed towards their expulsion (which it sometimes did in any event) – not as a response to a given event, but to deal with situations where court or tribunal processes were, he claimed, being overwhelmed, manipulated or abused, including by lawyers taking technicalities.[11]

Watchlists and other UK-entry and UK-exit mechanisms

The data that the e-Borders system collects about arrivals and departures also records a person's immigration status and related details. Staff dealing with UK visa applications overseas are thus able to check applications against that

---

[9] A fast track service is available to other applicants: see: www.ips.gov.uk
[10] Seemingly under the Royal prerogative rather than at Common Law.
[11] At one stage there was talk of 'technical defences, etc.' being outlawed!

database, e.g. concerning the credibility or veracity of applicants or their sponsors. Supported by biometrics (above), this is intended to enhance the overall effectiveness of entry clearance as time progresses. Passenger details (including names, dates of birth, nationality and travel document details) are checked against multi-agency 'watchlists' prior to boarding a flight. Under the 'Authority to Carry' scheme, the border staff are able to examine compulsory advance passenger information (API) and passenger name records (PNR),[12] to try and identify passengers who represent a risk to security or who might abuse border controls.

Consideration is being given by the Home Office to combining the e-Borders programme (above) with watchlists that are geared to the collection of fines and compensation ordered by the criminal courts (almost £500 million being outstanding as at mid-2007), fees for health treatment obtained by foreigners not entitled to use the UK National Health Service (NHS) (so-called 'health tourists' cost the UK some £9 million a year); generating 'no-fly lists' of people given to 'air rage' and other forms of on-board disruption; and to the collection of tax, national insurance and other public dues, including by better tracking of people claiming to be 'non-resident' or 'non-domiciled' in the UK and thus exempt from some or all of what would otherwise be UK tax liabilities of up to £2 billion a year. The idea appears to be that anyone owing such amounts will be obliged to pay or enter into arrangements for payment before being allowed to travel.[13]

IMMIGRATION

Immigration into the UK - entry by non-UK citizens seeking to remain here on a permanent basis - is controlled by law. But it is nowadays automatically open to a wide range of people including most people from the European Union, in addition to Commonwealth citizens as already intimated at the start of this chapter. Since the ending of the Cold War and the opening up of the former Eastern bloc large numbers of people have entered the UK; whilst discussion of immigration has become intertwined with that relating to citizenship, its ceremonies and Britishness[14] as noted at the end of this chapter.[15] Immigration

---

[12] Terms that have now entered the border control lexicon.

[13] The possibilities are endless – and worrying should there be less benign government.

[14] Further useful information re Britishness can be found at www.passportoffice.gov.uk

[15] Historically, the number of people coming to the UK was first estimated in the 'Emigration Report 1875', when it stood at 94,228 (it was thought to have been 49,157 in 1870; and, e.g. had risen to 185,799 by 1894).

control statistics confirm that the UK continues to have a net influx of migrants which stood at 185,000 in 2006.[16]

Immigrants (and asylum seekers) have been demonised from time-to-time as parasites, scroungers or criminals. Some members of the anti-immigration lobby have been dubbed 'Powellites', after the late political orator, Enoch Powell MP, who in 1968 spoke of seeing 'the River Tiber foaming with much blood' at the prospect of as many as 3.5 million Commonwealth citizens coming to the UK, something that still resonates in certain quarters. When he was home secretary, David Blunkett MP, was obliged to denounce certain campaigning groups promoting similarly 'racist' views and to accuse them of inflammatory behaviour. According to Oliver Letwin MP, the then Tory shadow Home Secretary: 'We should not end up thinking that people who seek to migrate are like robbers or villains or murderers. They are by and large perfectly good-natured people seeking to better themselves'.[17] But such exchanges highlight the need for balance and the fine line between immigration and asylum issues and the potential for racism, discrimination, hate and ultimately violence.

The UK Immigration Service (UKIS)

In April 2007 the UKIS evolved into the Border and Immigration Agency (BIA). Border staff (seemingly the modern description) now consider applications for permission to enter and remain in the UK, for asylum and for citizenship. This they do in line with a Home Office and Foreign Office-led international initiative, *Managing Global Migration: A Strategy to Build Stronger International Alliances to Manage Migration*, which sets out global plans to halt illegal immigration.[18] To the fore in this are partnerships with foreign governments and other UK government departments to speed up the return of people with no right to be in the UK. Through working with countries that regularly act as transit points along immigration routes, the UK has sought to place such issues further up the agenda internationally. This strategy has been developed jointly by the Home Office and the Foreign and Commonwealth Office, after close consultation with the Department for Trade and Industry and also with the Serious Organised Crime Agency (SOCA) (*Chapter 3*).

---

[16] Some 565,000 individuals intending to stay for one year, less the 385,000 who left the UK. Altogether, 50,000 people from Eastern Europe came to work in the UK in April, May and June of 2007 (6,000 down on 2006), mainly from Poland and other new EU states. Applications for permanent residence fell by 25 per cent in 2006 to 134,000. The figures appear at www.homeoffice.gov.uk/rds/immigration

[17] There is a proud tradition of lawful immigration into the UK and a 24 hour virtual Museum of Immigration and Diversity, an offshoot of its physical parent in Spitalfields (a historic location for waves of immigrants in the East End of London), known as '19 Princelet Street, E1 6QH': www.princeletstreet.org.uk

[18] (2007). See www.ind.homeoffice.gov.uk/6353/aboutus/internationalstrategy

'Illegal immigrant'

This is the everyday term that is usually applied to someone entering the UK without passing through immigration control, obtaining entry by deception (or not telling their whole story), overstaying his or her visa or, e.g. going on-the-run pending a decision on his or her removal from the UK.[19] Although widely used, some people consider the term 'illegal immigrant' to be deeply offensive.

In 2003, the Home Office admitted that it did not know – and perhaps could never know with any degree of certainty – how many 'illegal' immigrants there are in the UK; but indicated that some progress in this regard might be made if identity cards are introduced as noted in *Chapter 7*. In 2004, it was reported that 'more than 1,000' illegal immigrants had been arrested following random swoops on travellers on the London Underground, a total of 235 such operations were mounted over a period of 12 months. It was accompanied by what was described as a trawl for failed asylum seekers.

Many illegal immigrants are forced, through circumstances such as an absence of status as citizens and a need to remain 'invisible', to work under poor conditions and as part of the black economy, organized crime or in the sex industry. Cross-channel ferry and train operators are now obliged to co-operate with the Home Office including in terms of information and procedures or face financial charges under 'carrier's liability' laws (above); including by having effective controls in place, e.g. to prevent stowaways. The technology used by border staff includes heartbeat detectors, thermal imaging and gamma scanners, contributing to the discovery of 4,000 would-be illegal immigrants seeking to enter the UK from France alone in the first six months of these enhanced controls. Measures and targets have been introduced in an attempt to counter the destruction of travel, identity and other documents and refusals to co-operate with attempts at repatriation.

Immigration detention centres

'Immigration detention centres' (sometimes called 'holding centres' or 'removal centres' depending on their precise function and regime) is the term applied to establishments where foreigners can be detained pending the hearing or disposal of their cases: asylum seekers awaiting the outcome of their applications to enter the UK; foreign prisoners or people who are suspected of being illegal immigrants pending their removal, i.e. provided that they are not held in a normal prison or remand centre or returned forthwith to their country of origin. Such centres are administered by HM Prison Service[20] or on its behalf by private sector contractors (as is frequently the norm). The official figures show that this

---

[19] Sometimes the seemingly more neutral term 'migrant' is used; or at the opposite extreme such people may be referred to simply – and out of hand – as 'illegals'.

[20] Now a Ministry of Justice (MOJ) responsibility.

form of detention rose from around 900 in the mid-1990s to 1,750 in 2004. In mid-2007 it stood at 2,115 of which 1,435 were failed asylum seekers.[21]

Accommodation is not unlike that of an open prison, but there are also secure cells for dangerous offenders and other high-risk prisoners. The stock of such accommodation has been expanded in modern times to cope with a backlog of asylum applications and an increase in the numbers of foreign people seeking asylum.

There have been a number of serious disturbances at such centres often due to the fact that innocent asylum seekers have sensed that they were being treated as criminals or housed alongside them. There has also been what at one centre was described as 'a dislocation in casework handling' and a lack of attention to basic office disciplines and courtesies, such as answering faxes, returning telephone calls, checking information and giving regular updates. At Yarls Wood, Bedfordshire in 2002, large sections of the establishment were wrecked and many of the buildings raised to the ground by fire causing damage to a value of over £5 million; an 'explosion of violence' having begun after a woman detainee was pinned to the ground for ignoring instructions.[22] In 2003, five men were convicted of violent disorder and each sentenced to imprisonment for four years; the private sector operator being described as ill-equipped to deal with such an outbreak and the premises ill-adapted. Several other men were acquitted, and no-one was convicted of arson despite the fact that buildings were burned down.[23] Another riot occurred at Campsfield House Detention Centre, Oxfordshire in 1997 (again run by the private sector), but the trial collapsed after staff evidence was deemed unreliable. Controversial events have since occurred at Harmondsworth (near Heathrow Airport) (2006) and again at Campsfield House (2007) when 26 detainees – mostly convicted foreign prisoners awaiting deportation - went on-the-run following arson and other criminal damage.

---

[21] www.homeoffice.gov.uk/rds/immigration

[22] One of the most notorious border incidents ever involved a woman, Joy Gardner, a Jamaican overstayer aged 40 who died during restraint when immigration officers and police called at her home to deport her, the official cause of death being brain damage due to lack of oxygen. In 1995, three police officers stood trial for her manslaughter, but were acquitted. No disciplinary action was taken against these officers and a senior police officer was cleared of wrong-doing in disciplinary proceedings. The case still resonates, with others, and some detention deaths in custody, as featured at www.irr.org.uk In 2005, it was reported that private security firms involved in the removal of failed asylum seekers frequently face claims of assault, intimidation and sexual assault.

[23] Yarls Wood reopened in 2003.

Immigration status check

When someone arrives in the UK or at any time thereafter an immigration status check can be made, e.g. by border agency staff, or the police during a routine patrol or arrest, e.g. when someone is stopped for a road traffic offence. This can be done under new and largely unrestrained terrorism powers (*Chapter 5*), or the general police 'sus laws'. Such a check - which can nowadays be made virtually instantaneously by mobile telephone against a computer database - may itself lead to arrest and the subsequent involvement of the BIA. Since 2003 hospitals have been required to check the immigration status of suspicious patients under a crackdown on foreigners seeking National Health Service (NHS) treatment to which they are not entitled. Similarly, regulations and controls have been tightened re the activities of gang masters (offering work at low rates and often high risk to vulnerable illegal immigrants)[24] and against people traffickers.

The Asylum and Immigration Tribunal (AIT)

Often, foreign detainees are free to return to their own country rather than remain in detention or prison, but some may be asylum seekers fearing, e.g. torture there (see further under *Asylum*, below). The independent AIT, a Ministry of Justice (MOJ) responsibility, hears appeals against decisions made by the home secretary or his or her officials relating to asylum, immigration and nationality matters. The main types of appeal are made against decisions to refuse someone political asylum in the UK; refuse them entry to or leave to remain in the UK for permanent settlement; deport them from the UK; or to refuse entry to the UK for a family visit. Appeals are heard by one or more immigration judges, sometimes accompanied by non-legal members of the AIT; all appointed by the Lord Chancellor on the recommendation of the Judicial Appointments Commission and who form an independent judicial body. The judge or panel decides whether the appeal should be allowed or dismissed; the determination being provided in writing together with the reasons for it. In certain circumstances, either party can apply for reconsideration of the outcome.

The Special Immigration Appeals Commission (SIAC)

Superior court review of immigration decisions, i.e. by the higher judiciary, is normally the responsibility of the Special Immigration Appeals Commission (SIAC), again an MOJ responsibility and part of the Tribunals Service. Section 6 of the SIAC Act 1997 allows for a special advocate to be appointed to represent the interests of the appellant in an appeal hearing before SIAC. Rule 35 of the

---

[24] Notoriously re the 'Morecambe cockle pickers' when 23 illegal immigrants were drowned by an incoming tide as they worked resulting in a manslaughter conviction. There have been instances of would-be illegal immigrants suffocating *en masse* in airless transport containers or freezing to death in aircraft baggage holds or undercarriages.

SIAC Procedure Rules 2003 sets out the functions of a special advocate, namely to cross examine witnesses, make written submissions and to make oral submissions at hearings from which the appellant parties can be excluded.

Joint Council for the Welfare of Immigrants (JCWI)

The JCWI is an independent nationwide voluntary organization, campaigning for justice and combating racism in immigration and asylum law and policy. It provides free advice and casework, training courses, and a range of publications on issues such as visas, marriage rules and current and forthcoming legislation. It has an advice line that deals with specific queries on immigration, refugee or nationality issues which can be used from abroad via the British Embassy in a given country. JCWI also offers free legal advice on immigration, nationality and asylum matters to immigration law professionals and private individuals.[25]

Migrant Helpline

Migrant Helpline is a website dedicated to explaining and assisting asylum seekers and refugees; vulnerable people who come to the UK 'with a strong determination to rebuild their lives'. It is a charity involved with: providing advice and support for asylum seekers and refugees entering and living in the UK; facilitating the integration of asylum seekers and refugees into the community; and promoting awareness of asylum issues. The helpline provides information on the plight of asylum seekers and refugees. The reasons why people leave their own country and seek a new life in the UK are investigated; the stories of individuals who suffer persecution, discrimination, torture and hate crimes offer an insight into the misery and suffering they may have experienced under oppressive regimes and political and religious groups.[26]

Nationality Checking Service (NCS)

The NCS is a partnership between the Home Office, (the existing) Border and Immigration Agency (BIA) and local authorities. It allows people applying for British citizenship to make their applications, in person, at the office of their local council. For a modest fee, participating councils will check that applications are completed correctly and that they have been submitted with all the necessary supporting documents and the correct fee. A Nationality Group Call Centre also answers calls 'quickly and professionally' (0845 010 5200). In relation to naturalisation, stateless people or questions affecting 'right of abode', and according to complexity the NCS can take from six weeks to over six months.

---

[25] For further information, see www.jcwi.org.uk
[26] See www.migranthelpline.org.uk

ASYLUM

People trying to escape from oppression in their own countries but with no actual right of entry or abode in the UK have sought asylum in Great Britain across the centuries – Huguenots in the 16th and 17th centuries, Jews in the late 19th and early 20th centuries and again in the 1930s, Asians from East Africa in the 1960s and 1970s; contributing to the development of communities in many of the UK's larger cities in particular. Many such people have made important contributions to the UK's social, cultural and economic life, but may also have experienced a degree of prejudice and hostility. One modern-day issue is whether 'assurances' that people will not be abused if returned are a sufficient safeguard; the UK courts having ruled that these are not sufficient.[27]

In 2003, two asylum seekers convicted and sentenced to imprisonment for travelling on forged passports were awarded over £130,000 in damages against the Home Office by the High Court after their prosecution was found to have 'overlooked' a United Nations (UN) provision on the status of refugees banning such prosecutions. It is estimated that between 5,000 and 10,000 asylum seekers had already been convicted under that provision. The High Court has also ruled that the prosecution of asylum seekers for travelling on false papers is in breach of the UK's Obligations under the UN Refugee Convention (1951). According to Lord Justice Simon Brown, no one in the Criminal Justice System (CJS) had given the least thought to Article 31 of that convention which provides that asylum seekers are not to be penalised for entering a country illegally. Understandings as to what was considered to be the law had also caused defence lawyers to advise people that they had no real alternative but to enter a plea of guilty.

From 2004, the Government also signalled its intention of depriving all asylum seekers who fail to register in the UK of access to British schools and hospitals. Spending on legal aid for immigration and asylum cases is in the region of £200 million a year.[28] It has been said that whilst quotas can be imposed on immigration this is hardly the case with asylum seekers, since no-one can anticipate the potential terrors from which people may wish to flee.

In 2007, it was announced that consideration was being given to the idea of an amnesty for asylum seekers in order to clear a backlog of up to 450,000 'legacy cases', i.e. partly inherited from earlier administrations due to the fact that many people previously turned down for asylum – refused refugee status – were never actually expelled from the country; some of whom may now qualify for UK residency due to the time that has elapsed since that rejection. The asylum figures show that 6,780 failed asylum seekers (below) were removed from Britain

---

[27] The matter is yet to reach the House of Lords.
[28] The Law Society has even claimed that this squeezes the budget and distorts priorities.

in the first six months of that year; compared to 10,345 in the same period in 2006. New applications fell to the lowest level for some 15 years at 1,500 per month as against a total of 23,610 applicants across the whole of 2006, possibly a response to closer controls and scrutiny. The largest single groups of applicants are from Afghanistan and China. Some 25 per cent of applications succeed.[29]

DEPORTATION

Deportation is the enforced repatriation or transfer of a foreigner to his or her own country or a third, safe, country. It may thus only occur out of the UK in respect of a non-UK Citizen – but a UK citizen may be deported into the UK from abroad. It occurs where someone has entered a country unlawfully, represents a threat to national security, or is otherwise 'unwelcome'. The home secretary can act of his or her own motion to deport someone, or when a court has previously made a recommendation for deportation when imposing a sentence. Thus, ultimately, all deportation outcomes turn upon executive action rather than judicial action; although that action will be subject to judicial review, e.g. on the ground that it is unreasonable or that correct procedures were not followed, or on human rights grounds.

Deportation should be distinguished from refusal of entry to the UK, i.e. the situation whereby someone is turned back at a UK seaport or airport by border staff; from removal from the UK following an unsuccessful claim for asylum or a failed immigration check (above); or extradition (below). In modern times, issues have arisen, in particular: when recommendations for deportation have not been acted upon by the home secretary at the end of a sentence of imprisonment on a foreign person (*Chapter 1* and *10*); and concerning UK citizens deported from abroad to the UK by foreign government's whose records of offences abroad have not reached or been input into UK criminal record databases. The exchange of such information and the development of joined-up databases is now a priority within Europe, especially.

In accordance with the policy of the Home Office, all foreign national prisoners should be considered for deportation before being released from a sentence of imprisonment; including, as a matter of routine, all those given sentences of 12 months or more who are assessed as being likely to re-offend. This has not occurred in full measure: it was revealed in 2006 that 1,023 such prisoners had been released without assessments or consideration; 103 of these re

---

[29] www.homeoffice.gov.uk/rds/immigration

whom it was said no information was readily available in relevant files – a form of 'systemic failure'.[30]

EXTRADITION

Extradition is an executive process under which the home secretary can order that someone should be removed from the UK to face trial in another jurisdiction or because he or she is a fugitive from that country. There must be a reciprocal extradition treaty[31] in force vis-à-vis the state concerned (and with corresponding arrangements for extradition into the UK). Such orders are made on the application of the requesting state and can be challenged by way of judicial review. Since 11 September 2001, the procedures for cases involving allegations of terrorist offences (*Chapter 5*) have been reviewed, simplified and expedited. Extradition is arguably one of the most sensitive responsibilities that the home secretary has to exercise. In one *cause célèbre*, Jack Straw MP, when home secretary, refused to extradite General Pinochet, the former Chilean head-of-state, to Spain. The procedures work in reverse with foreign countries sending fugitives to the UK on application to them by the home secretary. Well-known fugitives from the UK, and illustrative of the difficulties sometimes encountered, include the 'Great Train Robber' Ronald Biggs who having escaped from prison in the UK then avoided extradition to the UK by remaining in Brazil due to parental responsibilities for many years before returning voluntarily to continue with a still to be served 30 year sentence. The former business tycoon Asil Nadir found a similar extradition-free haven in Northern Cyprus.

Certain requirements must normally be met before fugitives will be sent to another country where allegations have been made of offences. Thus, e.g. the offence that is charged must also be or approximate to an offence in the sending country, and - in the case of the UK - the home secretary must be satisfied that the accused will receive a fair trial and not, e.g. face capital punishment, torture or inhuman or degrading treatment.

---

[30] Included in this were a number of dangerous offenders, whose convictions included murder (3), rape (9) and sexual offences (48), some of a paedophile nature (5) and assault (including grievous bodily harm (GBH)) (50); triggering a nationwide manhunt and the resignation of then home secretary, Charles Clarke.

[31] Some imbalance in the notion of 'reciprocity' has been demonstrated by a number of USA requests that need not be based on specific or reasonable evidence, as in the case of Lord Black (extradited and convicted of fraud in the USA) and the so-called 'National Westminster Bank Three' (currently in prison in the USA awaiting trial for fraud there).

THE BORDER AND IMMIGRATION AGENCY (BIA)

In April 2007, the Immigration and Nationality Directorate of the Home Office became the BIA, a central aim of which is 'to manage immigration in the interests of Britain's security, economic growth and social stability' (Aim 6):

> We consider applications from people who want to come to the UK to work, do business, visit relatives, take a holiday or settle permanently. We manage routes into the UK labour market for people who want to work here, deciding applications for work permits and entry under other schemes. There are different programmes tailored to different levels of skill, but all designed to meet the changing needs of the UK economy.

As to nationality, the agency decides applications from people who want to become British citizens (below). As to asylum (above) the agency asserts:

> We are responsible for processing all claims for asylum and asylum support made in the UK. We determine applications from asylum seekers, granting five years leave to remain (LTR) to those who fears of persecution, integrating them swiftly into our society. We also provides accommodation and subsistence support to destitute asylum seekers while we consider their claims. Removing people from the UK when their claims fail is one of our priorities.

Concerning border control and entry clearance, in 2006:

> Our immigration officers facilitated the arrival of nearly 90 million passengers in the UK, more than 12 million of whom were subject to immigration control. Eurostar passengers now pass through UK immigration controls before they embark for the UK, and this has had a significant effect on the arrival of passengers without the correct documents. With the Foreign and Commonwealth Office, we run UK Visas. Working from British diplomatic posts overseas, UK Visas staff decide applications from people who need to get permission to enter the UK before they travel.

The agency's work is founded on four key objectives, i.e. 'to.

- strengthen our border, use tougher checks abroad so that only those with permission can travel to the UK, and ensure we know who leaves so that we can take action against those who break the rules;
- fast track asylum decisions, remove those whose claims fail and integrate those who need our protection;
- ensure and enforce compliance with our immigration laws, removing the most harmful people first and denying the privileges of Britain to those here illegally; and

- boost Britain's economy by bringing the right skills here from around the world, and ensuring this country is easy to visit legally.'

Stakeholders and inspection

At its web-site,[32] the BIA states that it is committed to developing and maintaining an open and constructive working relationship with all key stakeholders: 'We work closely with many diverse stakeholders, ranging from individuals and local community groups to larger bodies including the voluntary sector, local authorities, the police, legal bodies, international organisations, the education sector and other government departments'. Measures to simplify the workings of the BIA include streamlining the number of stakeholder groups working to it. Many were wound up in 2006 and a single Corporate Stakeholder Group (CSG) formed. The background to and the need for this were outlined an IND Review, *Getting it Right: Consulting Staff, Stakeholders and the Public.*[33] Also proposed in the review was the setting up of an independent inspectorate for immigration; the first stage of which has been a consultation document concerning the need for a single body to give a clear and consistent analysis of border matters rather than a range of monitoring, advisory and inspection bodies. The paper goes on to outline Government thinking on areas of immigration policy and operations that this body might examine, including effectiveness; quality of decision-making; enforcement powers; access to information; and the treatment of individuals. In conjunction with the Home Office, the CSG focuses on six key objectives:

- protecting the nation from terrorist attack;
- cutting crime, especially violent and drugs-related crime;
- enabling people to feel safer in their homes and daily lives, particularly through more visible, responsive and accountable local policing;
- rebalancing the criminal justice system in favour of the law abiding majority and the victim;
- managing offenders, to protect the public and reduce re-offending; and
- securing UK borders, preventing abuse of immigration laws and managing migration 'to boost the UK'.

CITIZENSHIP AND BRITISHNESS

The UK's first official citizenship ceremony for people taking British nationality took place at Brent Town Hall, north-London in 2004, since when such

---

[32] www.ind.homeoffice.gov.uk
[33] Immigration and Nationality Directorate, 2006.

ceremonies have become a regular feature of obtaining UK citizenship.[34] Now, they are often seen as part of a move to encourage 'Britishness'; with applicants obliged to take a citizenship test, described in *Life in the United Kingdom: A Journey to Citizenship*[35], that is aimed at people wishing to settle in the UK. A new 2007 test requires people to answer written questions based on chapters with headings such as: 'A Changing Society', 'The UK Today: A Profile', 'How the UK is Governed', 'Everyday Needs' and 'Employment'. New guidelines have been introduced for applications for naturalisation and the registration of minors (children under the age of 18), intended to provide easy and more comprehensive advice on how to make a successful application and pass the test. The nationality regulations also now include the extension of a good character requirement to all applicants aged ten or over. Checks include enquiries of the police, the security services and HM Revenue and Customs. Any outstanding police action must be notified to the Home Office whilst an application for naturalisation is under consideration.

Identity checking (see, generally, *Chapter 7*) is being enhanced to reduce fraudulent applications including via the use of passport style photographs and endorsement by the referee; with checks also being carried out to ensure that referees are qualified in law to act.; and also that someone else is not sitting the citizenship test, re which there have been a number of prosecutions. Clear warnings have also been issued about the consequences of fraud in general and unacceptable behaviour towards test centre personnel.

Britishness

Since the early 2000s a sense has been growing that the formerly prevailing idea of multi-culturalism – a situation in which diversity and difference and a range of different cultures were encouraged to co-exist – was having a separatist effect; that multi-culturalism militates against any coherent or overall sense of Britishness. Naturally, such discussion is always likely to be contentious and some people may see such ideas as discriminatory or as critical of race or religion. It might also be objected that appeals to patriotism always risk an excess of patriotism and xenophobia; so that the ills that they are intended to reduce are overwhelmed by factors of a worse kind. Whatever the broader debate,

---

[34] Hence the phenomenon of private sector ventures such as www.britishness-test.co.uk and www.newuktest.co.uk aimed at people sitting the 'Life in the UK Test'. The former describes itself as: 'The first website to introduce the Online Interactive Training for Life in the UK Test. Our experienced trainers currently teach people English and prepare them ... Questions are prepared so that they are challenging and keep students focused ... to suit people of all calibres ... We always review our question bank ... to keep them current and relevant ... We have extensive knowledge of the Life in the UK test'.

[35] Home Office (2007). With transitional arrangements re students of a previous version.

'Britishness' is now firmly part of the UK administration's agenda and especially since mid-2007. Immediately before becoming prime minister, Gordon Brown (then still chancellor of the exchequer) spoke at a seminar on Britishness at the Commonwealth Club, London, in May 2007 saying 'what a pleasure it is to be here at this discussion on our country's character, our values, our future':

> I am here to listen, I am here to learn and I am here because I want to discuss with you during the course of the day what you think about being British, how important being British is to your identity, what you think characterises us as the British, what in particular could be said to be British values, what are the British values that make us proud to be British.

Describing this as a 'renewed focus', he went on to consider such matters as whether all the different countries of the union that makes up the UK - Scotland, Wales, England and Northern Ireland - want to stay part of that union as well as:

- how we better integrate our ethnic communities and respond to migration;
- how we respond to Muslim fundamentalism;
- what is our role in Europe and the European constitution; and
- whether global challenges demand a stronger sense of national purpose.[36]

Britishness and the issues surrounding it is also a central feature of the Green Paper, *The Governance of Britain* and the work of the MOJ.[37]

---

[36] Further extracts from this key address appear in *Appendix III* to this work.
[37] See the companion to this work, *The New Ministry of Justice*.

Safeguarding Personal Identity

CHAPTER 7

Safeguarding Personal Identity

Safeguarding personal identity is one of the Home Office's key objectives as noted in *Chapter 1*. Only a decade ago, such an aim might have provoked puzzlement or not been understood at all. Certain offenders or people trying to enter the UK illegally have always sought to pass themselves off as someone else, or to otherwise misrepresent their identity for the purpose of various forms of dishonesty. The difference in the modern-day is the sheer speed of events, global mobility, the rise of the internet with the possibilities that this provides for cyber-crime committed on a grand scale, including theft, fraud and other kinds of deception. Hence one response of Government: the desirability of identity cards as one means of tackling such abuses and making subjects or targets easier to trace (whilst at the same time helping in the fight against terrorism) (*Chapter 6*). Just as scientific advances allow the police or other agents of law enforcement to obtain evidence, arrests and convictions (*Chapters 3* and *8*), so too do new possibilities play into the hands of criminals.

Identification
Identification of an individual or thing is an integral part of many criminal justice processes, whether of people, objects, documents, e.g. so as to ensure that the correct person is the subject of an arrest, charge, remand, prosecution or sentence; to establish who the victim or a witness is; and requires the uniqueness or original nature of a certificate, statement or exhibit. It is a formal part of what might be described as everyday chains of evidence. Thus, a suspect might be identified by a witness from a line of people of people who look like him or her at a police 'identification parade', or singled out as a target for questioning or surveillance as part of an ongoing inquiry or investigation. The shooting dead by mistake of John Charles de Menezes noted in *Chapter 5* shows what a fallible process this can be; and there are sufficient miscarriage of justice cases to indicate why special rules and codes of practice have been developed by the police and courts to reduce the risk that an innocent person may be arrested or convicted.

Other techniques include, e.g. the science of fingerprinting; DNA-testing (sometimes called genetic fingerprinting); checking against dental records; looking for birthmarks, scars, etc.; and comparison with existing records and offence or offender profiles giving someone's *modus operandi*.[1] The identikit was once the leading method of creating an image of (usually) a suspect from a selection of drawings of standard facial characteristics on printed cards or acetate slides; now largely superseded by the photofit and computer programmes that allow virtually infinite adjustment and manipulation of facial images on a screen. These are then compared with a 'Rogues Gallery' of known offenders or suspects in an album held by the police, increasingly also an electronic utility. In modern times, face recognition technology allows facial images captured by CCTV (*Chapters 3* and *8*) to be compared instantly with millions of similar stored electronic pictures; although this technology is still in its infancy. Similarly, schemes of electronic vehicle number plate recognition now connect the police directly to the databases of the Driver and Vehicle Licensing Agency (DVLA) and private insurers of vehicles; and thus to the driver or keeper of a vehicle.

Names and identification
'Name' and 'identity' are not always co-terminous. The latter concerns who someone is; the former merely what a person is generally known as or called by other people. In the UK and in everyday practical terms, identification processes are perhaps less effective than in many countries due to the fact that people may use whatever name they like provided that this is not for the purposes of fraud. Many offenders use an alias, whilst other people, especially professional people may use a maiden or former name, or a pseudonym, pen-name or stage name. Within an already loose situation, people can change their name at will and with little formality (should they even wish to formalise matters at all). A similar problem applies to business or corporate identity although this has been tackled to a greater extent. For example in 2005, Companies House, the responsible agency, reported that it was working in partnership with the police to prevent the theft of corporate identities in scams involving unauthorised alteration of company addresses by a third party.[2] Such scams rely on goods being delivered to a false address before the real company discovers that its details have been changed. It is said that some £50 million a year is lost to such simple frauds.

Some of the resistance to the idea of identity cards in the UK would appear to be driven by the same factor that causes sensitivity about someone's name: privacy, especially insofar as casual transactions with other people such as shopkeepers are concerned, almost along the lines: 'I don't need to tell you who I am/my business: that's for me to know and you to find out'! Nonetheless, the move to identity cards may alter this: in the rest of Europe (or the USA) where it

---

[1] There really is no limit to this, e.g. in 2003 a victim whose body had been dismembered and decomposed and where no DNA-match, fingerprints, etc. were possible was identifiable only by the serial numbers of her breast implants.

[2] Operation Sterling.

can be a criminal offence not to carry an identity card and answer questions related to identification if asked to do so by the police, most people would find it strange that no such documentation is required in the UK.

Fresh identity

A 'new identity', i.e. a new name and background[3] may be provided to an offender, supergrass, ex-prisoner, witness, etc. by a police Protection Unit or similar scheme; as it may to a serving prisoner by HM Prison Service where he or she is being held apart from other prisoners on Rule 43 for his or her own safety. Prisoners frequently adopt a new 'identity' in this same sense on their release from prison in order to make a fresh start (or sometimes to avoid the further attention of the authorities).[4] Changes may then also be made in public records.

DNA-testing

In modern times, the most reliable method of non-visual identification of a suspect, other person or item is nowadays by means of DNA-testing. Not only is DNA-testing used by scenes of crime officers (SOCOs) and forensic experts and the Forensic Science Service (FSS)[5] in relation to current investigations but also in relation to cold cases, many of which are being solved following the taking of samples from people who have been arrested for routine offences and as police powers of arrest have become easier and wider (see further *Chapter8*).

IDENTITY THEFT AND IDENTITY FRAUD

Pretending to be someone else – a device as old as crime itself – was always the stock-in-trade of the habitual fraudster, con-man, spiv, wide boy, hotel bilker or occasional opportunist offender.[6] In common parlance, 'identity theft' (or often just 'ID theft') or 'identity fraud' refer to the adopting of the name and details of someone else for the purposes of committing an offence such as obtaining the transfer of funds from a bank or building society account or by charging expenditure to it, especially over the internet. It can take other forms and may be accompanied by false documents (e.g. a forged passport or someone else's driving licence that may have been stolen). In terms of the internet, with its capacity for remoteness and anonymity, it is now so wide-scale as to demand the

---

[3] Sometimes called a 'legend'.

[4] Sex offenders are limited in this due, e.g. to the Sex Offender Register, licence conditions.

[5] Forensic Science Services (FSS) is a trading name of Forensic Science Service Ltd., a UK Government owned company: *Chapter 8*. It was formerly a Home Office function.

[6] Such, e.g. as the person who happens on and cashes someone else's misdirected state benefits cheque; or the accidental recipient of some else's property.

constant efforts of computer security experts to combat it.[7] It attracts the lone fraudster and organized crime alike to a virtual world in which crimes can be committed remotely and anonymously and which is so largely free from regulation or censorship that it has been dubbed 'The New Wild West', often free from ordinary forms of policing.[8] It is in such a context that the Home Office has linked aims of safeguarding identity and protecting the privileges of citizenship.

In 2007, internet-based identity fraud and identity theft was one of the fastest growing types of offence with an annual value approaching £2 billion.[9] For the private sector it is the single most important threat against which security measures need to be taken, hence such developments as the Credit Industry Fraud Avoidance System (CIFAS); warnings to the public about bin-pilfering (searching through refuse bins for personal data); and a new market in personal paper shredders. Hence also the Personal Identification Number (PIN).

According to the Home Office,[10] the terms 'identity theft' or 'identity fraud' are often used quite loosely to describe any situation in which personal details are misappropriated for gain. The following definitions have been developed by the Identity Fraud Steering Committee (IFSC) to clarify the terms:

1 Identity crime is a generic term for identity theft, creating a false identity or committing identity fraud.
2 False identity is:
   (a) a fictitious (i.e. invented) identity; or
   (b) an existing (i.e. genuine) identity that has been altered to create a fictitious identity.
3 Identity theft occurs when sufficient information about an identity is obtained to facilitate identity fraud, irrespective of whether, in the case of an individual, the victim is alive or dead.
4 Identity fraud occurs when a false identity or someone else's identity details are used to support unlawful activity, or when someone avoids an obligation or liability by falsely claiming that he or she was the victim of identity fraud.

These Home Office definitions are the ones used when assessing the extent of identity crime in the UK. They are not legal definitions nor tied to definitions of

---

[7] Computers need private sector security systems, especially if monetary transactions are involved. Conspiracy theorists argue that viruses, etc. are created to generate sales.
[8] It is also sometime associated with cyber-terrorism: setting-off computer viruses or frauds for political similar, including to cause anti-capitalist losses.
[9] According to the Home Office Identity Fraud Steering Committee (IFSC) (see later in this chapter) following a one-off exercise to update earlier Cabinet Office estimates for the purpose of establishing trends over the three years to 2007. The latest 'best estimate' was that identity fraud was already costing the UK economy some £1.7 billion a year.
[10] www.identity-theft.gov.uk

existing offences; and they apply to both individual and to corporate identity crime of the kind already noted above. Again, according to the Home Office:

> Examples of identity fraud include using a false identity or someone else's identity details (e.g. his or her name, address, previous address, date of birth, etc.) for commercial, economic or monetary gain; or obtaining goods or information; or obtaining access to facilities or services (such as opening a bank account, applying for benefit or obtaining a loan/credit card).

The IFSC have also developed definitions of corporate identity crime along parallel lines. Again, the Home Office stresses that these are evaluative tools and not legal definitions, etc. Examples of corporate identity fraud include using a false corporate identity or another company's identity details for commercial, economic or monetary gain; or obtaining goods or information; or obtaining access to facilities or services.

The Home Office Identity Fraud Steering Committee (IFSC)

The IFSC is a collaboration between UK financial bodies, government and the police to combat the threat of identity theft. It comprises representatives of:

- APACS - the UK bank payment association;
- Association of Chief Police Officers (ACPO) (see *Chapter 3*);
- British Bankers' Association;
- CIFAS, the UK Fraud Prevention Service;
- Department of Work and Pensions/Jobcentre Plus;
- Driver and Vehicle Licensing Agency (DVLA);
- Finance and Leasing Association;
- Financial Services Authority (FSA);
- HM Revenue and Customs;
- Home Office;
- Identity and Passport Service (IPS) (now part of the Borders and Immigration Agency)(see *Chapter 6*);
- Ministry of Justice (MOJ) (*Chapter 1*);
- Serious Organised Crime Agency (SOCA) (*Chapter 3*); and the
- Telecommunications UK Fraud Forum.

Home Office advice on identity theft

The existence of a Home Office identity theft web-site devised by the IFSC is a key example of how the Home Office is working to safeguard personal identity. It advises visitors about the intrinsic value of personal details and information. The following extracts from that information also give an impression of the nature of modern-day identity theft concerns and issues:

Criminals can find out your personal details and use them to open bank accounts and get credit cards, loans, state benefits and documents such as passports and driving licenses in your name ...

Criminals commit identity theft by stealing your personal information. This is often done by taking documents from your rubbish or by making contact with you and pretending to be from a legitimate organisation. .... Identity theft can result in fraud affecting your personal financial circumstances, as well as costing government and financial services millions of pounds a year. If your identity is stolen, you may have difficulty getting loans, credit cards or a mortgage until the matter is sorted out ... The following tips will help you protect your identity and prevent criminals from committing fraud in your name:

- Your identity and personal information are valuable assets. Keep them secure.
- Regularly obtain a copy of your personal credit file from one of the three credit reference agencies to see which financial organisations have accessed your details. It is particularly helpful to check your personal credit file two to three months after you have moved house.
- Be extra careful if you live in a property where other people could have access to your mail. In some cases a bank or credit card company could arrange for you to collect valuable items such as new plastic cards or cheque books from a local branch.
- If you suspect your mail is being stolen, contact the Royal Mail Customer Enquiry Line: 08457 740 740. Check whether a mail redirection order has been made in your name without your knowledge.
- If you move house, tell your bank, card issuer and all other organisations that you deal with immediately. Ask the Royal Mail to redirect any mail from your old address to your new one for at least a year.
- Consider using the Mailing Preference Service to limit the amount of unwanted mail you receive.
- Keep all your plastic cards safe
- If your plastic cards are lost or stolen, cancel them immediately. Keep a note of the emergency numbers you should call. Further details can be found at the Card Watch website.
- When giving your card details or personal information over the phone, Internet or in a shop, make sure other people cannot hear or see your personal information.
- Never carry documents or plastic cards unnecessarily. When not in use keep them in a safe place.
- Keep your documents safe
- Keep your personal documents in a safe place, preferably in a lockable drawer or cabinet at home. Consider storing valuable financial documents such as share certificates with your bank.
- If your passport or driving licence has been lost or stolen contact the issuing organisation immediately.

- Don't throw away entire bills, receipts, credit-or debit-card slips, bank statements or even unwanted post in your name. Destroy unwanted documents, preferably by using a shredder.
- Check statements as soon as they arrive. If any unfamiliar transactions are listed, contact the company concerned immediately.
- Keep your passwords and PINs safe.
- Never give personal or account details to anyone who contacts you unexpectedly. Be suspicious even if they claim to be from your bank or the police. Ask for their phone number, check it is genuine and, if so, call them back. Be aware that a bank will never ask for your PIN or for a whole security number or password. Keep them secure.
- Don't use the same password for more than one account and never use banking passwords for any other websites. Using different passwords increases security and makes it less likely that someone could access any other accounts.
- Keep your passwords safe and never record or store them in a manner which leaves them open to theft, such as in your purse or wallet.
- If you receive a suspicious e-mail purporting to be from a bona fide institution which requests personal details [advice is provided by the banking industry].

Another government web-site[11] gives advice on how to stay safe online when shopping, banking or doing business over the internet, and how to protect a computer and the personal information that it contains. This includes advice about how to dispose of unwanted computers (that may contain data on their hard disc). This particular web-site has been developed by the Government, police and the private sector. Concerning corporate identity fraud, the web-site offers dedicated advice emphasising that companies and their directors can also fall victim to identity fraud in person:

> Criminals can seek to commit corporate identity fraud in a variety of different ways, including by fraudulently changing a company's registered details at Companies House. Companies House has a three point plan to help companies protect against corporate identity fraud and safeguard the personal information of their directors. This involves filing information online (WebFiling), signing up to submitting all papers online (PROOF), and subscribing to an alert system that notifies companies when changes to their details are made (Monitor).[12]

It also offers advice on protecting the identity of deceased family members and 'things to look out for that also demonstrates how what would formerly have

---

[11] www.getsafeonline.org.uk

[12] More information about these dedicated services and combatting corporate identity fraud can be found at www.companieshouse.gov.uk

been initially a 'police matter' is now to be investigated at the outset largely by private sector banks and similar institutions, viz:

> If you believe you are a victim of identity fraud which has involved the use of plastic cards (such as credit and debit cards), online banking, or cheques, the matter should be reported by the account holder directly to the financial institution concerned. They will then be responsible for undertaking further verification and investigation, and, as appropriate, reporting cases of criminal activity directly to the police where they will be recorded and subsequent investigation considered. It should be noted that this process is applicable to England, Wales and Northern Ireland only ... These changes to the reporting of plastic card, online banking and cheque fraud were introduced by the Home Office on 1 April 2007, following discussion with the Association of Chief Police Officers (ACPO) and the financial sector, to reduce the level of bureaucracy involved in fraud recording, and to streamline the reporting and initial investigation of such frauds ...

The advice also recommends other precautions that citizens can take including by using the CIFAS Protective Registration Service.[13] Other cooperative ventures include the Home Office, Identity and Passport Service (below), and DVLA working together with APACS, FLA and CIFAS to support a project to produce *Identity Fraud: The UK Manual*.[14] The manual which typifies the extensive guidance, investment and interest in this topic within the private sector is designed to improve the training being provided to those in the financial sector responsible for checking customers' identities to ensure consistency and greater accuracy in verifying identity. It includes examples of known security features from UK passports and driving licences and provides advice to organizations to help spot forgeries and other identity scams.

New legislation
The Identity Cards Act 2006 created offences relating to possession, control and intent to use false identity documents, including a genuine document that relates to someone else. The statute applies to all identity documents, including identity cards to be issued under the NIS scheme (above), passports, immigration documents and driving licences, including driving licences, passports and identity cards issued by other countries. The Fraud Act 2006 which came into force in January 2007 created a new offence of fraud that can be committed in three ways: by making a false representation (dishonestly, with intent to make a gain, cause loss or risk of loss to another), by failing to disclose information and

---

[13] CIFAS Protective Registration may be placed by individuals against their own address when they have good reason to believe it may be used by a fraudster, e.g. when a passport has been stolen. For further information, see www.cifas.org.uk
[14] Card Watch (2007); see, also, www.cardwatch.org.uk

by abuse of position. Offences were also created of obtaining services dishonestly, possessing equipment to commit frauds, and making or supplying articles for use in frauds.

The Police and Justice Act 2006 contains a number of provisions to help prevent impersonation of deceased persons. Section 13 of the 2006 Act provides the General Register Office with the power to supply 'deceased person information'[15] to the police, Serious and Organised Crime Agency (SOCA), special police forces, and any other bodies specified by the home secretary in regulations for the prevention, detection, investigation and prosecution of offences. The Criminal Justice Act 2003 changed the law to align the penalty associated with fraudulently obtaining a driving licence with that of fraudulently obtaining a passport and made these arrestable offences. The maximum penalty with regard to either document is now imprisonment for two years.

Prosecution

In December 2005, a network of Single Points of Contact (SPOC) for prosecuting identity related crimes was established, with representatives from all police forces in England and Wales (*Chapter 3*) and a range of government departments and intelligence agencies. Each SPOC centre acts as a focal point for dealing with identity fraud and representatives are proactive with regard to pursuing identity related fraud and related offences across the agencies. The role also involves monitoring cases from the outset to conclusion and providing information and assistance to member agencies in combating identity fraud; leading to better co-ordination and, it is claimed, more successful prosecutions.

PASSPORTS AND IDENTITY FRAUD

The Identity and Passport Service (IPS) has deployed a database of lost and stolen passports. This is being shared with the border authorities (see, generally, *Chapter 6*) through Europol and Interpol to help detect and prevent identity fraud. A passport validation service is now available to public and private sector organisations. It involves checking passports against the passport database when they are presented as evidence of identity, e.g. when opening a bank account. As already indicated in *Chapter 6*, authentication of the identity of individuals by interview of all first time adult passport applicants has been introduced. IPS and DVLA also work closely together to establish higher standards of identity checking before they issue passports and driving licences.

---

[15] Popular intrigue has existed ever since Frederick Forsyth's novel, *The Day of the Jackal*, in which a hit-man takes his 'identity' from the headstone of the grave of someone who would have been his or her age. There have been several prosecutions in which copy-cat versions or variants of this method of obtaining a new identity have been uncovered.

Miscellaneous Home Office Responsibilities

CHAPTER 8

Miscellaneous Home Office Responsibilities

Following the split in the Home Office which led to the creation of the Ministry of Justice (MOJ), a considerable number of agencies, advisory groups and sponsored organizations now look to the MOJ rather than the Home Office. But even after jettisoning major and distracting responsibilities such as prisons, probation and its lead role in criminal policy-making, the Home Office is left with a wide range of tasks outside policing and border control. These include its interests in relation to scientific and technological advances, and research and development. It also has a major interest in advising other groups or services whose work underpins and informs its own policies. Many local or charitable services take their lead from the Home Office or rely on funding or other kinds of official support. Other Home Office concerns such as the drugs, guns or knives noted in this chapter show the Home Office setting a policy or strategy lead so as to bring the agencies together and facilitate work by various mainly external networks and partnerships.

SCIENCE AND TECHNOLOGY

The impact of developments in science and technology in relation to the work of the Home Office and its partner organizations are touched upon in earlier chapters.[1] Their application to crime, public saftey and border controls is also identified in the *Preface* to this book as one of the key reasons for using the term 'new Home Office'. Advances in science and technology are vital tools in the fight against crime, just as they can alter the way and ease with which crime can be committed. Diverse modern-day examples of such developments include:

- more effective methods of gathering evidence at the scene of a crime, including in relation to fingerprints and DNA;
- high powered, specialist equipment for the purposes of remote and covert surveillance and monitoring operations;
- improved systems to scan for weapons, explosives, drugs, people and animals, including x-ray machines, laser-based ultrasound technology and heat seeking equipment that may, e.g. locate a human being who is being trafficked or single out premises used for drug cultivation;

---

[1]   See, in particular, *Chapters 1, 3, 5* and *6*.

- the potential of global satellite positioning equipment or mobile telephone records, allowing searches, tracking of events, vehicles, people and animals, or their being recorded at a given place at a given time;
- more sophisticated forms of body armour (now often lighter than ever before) to protect police officers and members of the security services and the provision of 'less lethal weapons' such as Taser-guns;[2]
- modern-day and often instantaneous communications equipment and databases that give the advantage of speed over offenders;
- DNA-testing techniques and the national DNA-database that has already made an enormous contribution in detecting serious crime;
- the use of computer programmes to carry out their own 'fishing expeditions' thereby identifying suspects from profiles fed into the computer programme and its linked databases, a process that is proving particularly effective in relation to financial frauds, tax evasion, customs offences, VAT or carousel frauds, drug trafficking and people trafficking and other aspects of organized crime by tracking international movements;
- the tracing of suspects from lifestyle details retained by internet service providers or on the hard disc of a computer, as has been used when tracing paedophiles via their credit card details or people downloading indecent images of children; and
- access to a modern, responsive Forensic Science Service (below).

Science and Innovation Strategy 2005-2008

This provides the framework for the Home Office vision for the use and development of science and innovation in the fight against crime. The purpose of the strategy is to ensure that the Home Office uses science and technology to improve the effectiveness and efficiency of its work and to help drive future innovation. The expressed aim is to provide high quality science and technology 'that is fit for clearly defined purposes':

Quality is vital and our strategy is to have rigorous quality review processes for all Home Office science and technology. Where possible we will open all science and technology to external quality review processes. Where this is not possible, mainly for security reasons, we will use independent peer review from within the department or from other government departments. We must also be innovative and open if we are to achieve our aim of high quality science that is fit for its purpose. This openness about our science and technology requires us to positively encourage critical engagement with the external science and technology community to help drive

---

[2] A stun gun that remains controversial and that is the subject of legal test cases in other jurisdictions as having a, nonetheless, lethal capacity.

innovation. It also means that we must work creatively with technology suppliers to deliver innovation.[3]

Forensic science

Forensic science (or simply 'forensics') is the term applied to the application of scientific study and techniques to evidence or events in the sense that it seeks to establish, by expert and where possible incontrovertible, means whether or not something is a fact. In other situations an expert opinion may be expressed by a specialist who has examined whatever materials or information exist and applied these to rigorous professional assessments. Such investigations, conclusions or opinions may be applied, e.g. to the examination of a human body, blood, semen, a building, motor vehicle, compounds, drugs, guns and explosives (a special branch of forensics known as 'ballistics'), a building or minute particles of dust not visible to the naked eye or a sample of scrapings. There are few limits to the possibilities other than the state of scientific or technological knowledge at any given time, as to which and vis-à-vis crime and terrorism in particular, the Home Office seeks to be at the fore.

Forensics can be used, in particular, by pathologists to determine the cause of someone's death or by police investigators in order to link a crime to the offender. The Home Office has standing arrangements for liaison with, e.g. Forensic Science Service, Research Councils, and the forensic science and pathology communities. A forensic pathology unit within the Home Office itself oversees the provision of forensic pathology services in England and Wales and publishes documents for forensic pathologists to assist them in developing national competencies and standards for pathologists to adhere to. Expert opinion may need to be given as evidence in a trial when it can be tested by cross-examination[4] or the countervailing opinion of another expert who gives evidence for the defence and who may try to convince the court that the prosecution evidence is scientifically unsound.[5] In the majority of cases such prosecution evidence is conclusive and leads to a timely guilty plea because once the scientific facts are known the accused person has no real answer.

---

[3] www.homeoffice.gov.uk/documents/science-strategy

[4] Questions put to the expert, usually by a defence barrister or solicitor.

[5] A number of notorious 'cot death' opinions by the leading paediatrician Sir Roy Meadow led to several miscarriages of justice; and he was struck-off by the General Medical Council (GMC) before being reinstated with the remainder of his greater reputation restored. Other miscarriages have been corrected after confession statements were shown to be false when in some instances police officers were convicted and sent to prison: see, generally, the comments on police corruption in *Chapter 3*.

Forensic Science Services (FSS)

FSS is a trading name of Forensic Science Service Ltd, a UK Government owned company;[6] which describes itself as 'the market leader in the supply of forensic science services to police forces in England and Wales'. It is also a source of training, consultancy, and scientific support for overseas police forces and security services as well as the private sector. Historically the FSS was part of the Home Office (except that the Metropolitan Police Service had its own laboratory); it then became an executive agency and was privatised in 2005 but the FSS's former responsibilities for the National DNA-database (see later in this chapter) were retained by the government. The FSS has always been in the vanguard of such developments with a sound reputation for integrity, impartiality and accuracy, including internationally. It has some eleven facilities in the UK that are used by police forces nationwide (and to an extent overseas).

KEY DEVELOPMENTS IN RELATION TO DNA

Nowadays, in particular, forensic science frequently involves the use of DNA technology[7] to investigate crimes and accidents. DNA is the genetic code found in every cell in the body of a human being, animal or plant. Someone's (or something's) DNA is unique and it can thus be used to identify people, etc. with a degree of certainty and relative infallibility unknown in the past. DNA derived from samples taken from crime scenes or from individuals held in police custody can be searched against the records held in the national DNA database. This use of DNA technology has made a significant contribution to detecting serious crime. A DNA match on the database can, e.g.:

- point to the possible identity of an offender, with a high level of certainty;
- help to solve 'cold cases' – unsolved crimes possibly from many years ago;
- help identify serious offenders who are arrested for a routine offence when their DNA, which is now automatically taken on arrest, is found to match a DNA-profile that is already held on the National DNA-database (below);
- eliminate individuals from an inquiry or investigation and from suspicion with a degree of certainty if their DNA does not match that found at a crime scene or in a sample that has been retained by the police.

The discovery of DNA together with practical and now everyday forensic 'DNA-testing' has forged a revolution in techniques of detection and investigation – and led to a quantum leap in the way convictions are obtained. DNA evidence is

---

[6] Known as a GovCo. 'Privatisation' in this chapter should be so read.
[7] DNA stands for deoxyribonucleic acid.

relevant and available. Increasingly, DNA matches[8] help to solve cases of murder, manslaughter, other homicides, assaults, rape and other sexual offences. Key developments include the creation of a 'National DNA Database' (below), refinements in the scientific processes for locating, collecting and sampling DNA; and a broadening of those situations in which DNA can be required from a citizen as a matter of routine (as when someone is arrested for whatever reason) or as part of a specific investigation. Such possibilities have been enhanced with the developments in relation to 'low copy DNA' (poor quality DNA that can now be enhanced or 'grown') and the use of 'familial-DNA' (that of blood relative).[9] The odds against error from duplication are millions to one; and improve with every refinement.

In cases where DNA was discovered, the crime detection rate rose from 26 per cent to 40 per cent from 2004 to 2005. In a typical month suspects are now linked to 26 murders, 57 rapes and sexual offences and 3,000 motor vehicle, property and drug crimes. Over 40,000 samples and 4,000 'crime stain samples' are loaded on the DNA-database (below) every month. The annual number of crimes detected where DNA scene-to-suspect links were made quadrupled from 8,612 in 1999/2000 to 35,605 in 2004/05. The number of DNA crime scene to suspect matches increased by 75 per cent from 23,021 to 40,169 between 1999/2000 and 2004/05. The government and police forces have invested over £300 million in the database; and there are some 3,000 database matches each month; over 40,000 in 2004/05.[10] In 2005/6, 45,000 crimes were matched against records on the DNA-database; including 422 homicides and 645 rapes.[11]

Cold cases
Many previously stale cases are now being solved where the file was originally marked 'closed' or otherwise placed aside as not meriting the resources demanded by continuing with an investigation which would be prone to diminishing returns. In most instances – and especially with regard to high profile, serious or otherwise disturbing cases – arrangements now exist for a periodic review or re-examination to be undertaken; often by a different police officer, team or unit from that which conducted the original investigation; including from an outside police force. Also, several older 'miscarriage of justice'

---

8   Also known as a 'hit'.
9   The first instance (also a 'cold case') being the so-called Dearne Valley Rapist (2006). It is also a good example of the sheer power of DNA. James Lloyd (50) (aka 'the shoe rapist': he stored victims' shoes) was a serial rapist convicted at Sheffield Crown Court of four rapes and two attempts and sentenced to life imprisonment. The attacks were all part of a 'reign of terror' in the Dearne Valley area of South Yorkshire in the 1980s but for some 20 years all this had remained invisible.
10 Figures quoted by the Police Information Technology Organisation (PITO).
11 Home Office.

cases have been resolved by modern-day DNA-testing.[12] Simultaneously with such developments, there has been a change in the historic double jeopardy rule under which someone could not be tried twice for the self-same offence, even where there was fresh and convincing evidence, so that an accused person may now be tried a second time for certain serious 'qualifying offences'; possibly on the basis of DNA-based evidence that can now itself be enhanced: above.[13]

The National DNA-database

This is a nationwide database of DNA-profiles maintained by the National Identification Service (NIS) (under the general oversight of a Home Office board: below). It holds around four million DNA-profiles;[14] that are added to every time that a sample is found at a crime scene or taken at a police station, it being nowadays a standard practice for police forces to input such profiles to the database, making it a key police intelligence tool. According to the Home Office, it helps to:

- quickly identify offenders;
- make earlier arrests;
- secure more convictions; and
- provide critical investigative leads for police investigations.

Home Office oversight of the DNA-database

A Home Office unit is responsible for regulating the database. This work is overseen by a board composed of the Home Office, the Association of Chief Police Officers (ACPO) and the Association of Police Authorities (APA). The Human Genetics Commission is also represented on the board, and there are plans to establish an ethics group to contribute and offer advice. The government took control of the database from the Forensic Science Service (FSS) above in

---

[12] A famous instance is that of James Hanratty, executed at Bedford Prison for the A6 murder in 1962; whose DNA was found to be on the original trial exhibits (though his supporters continue to argue that they have been cross-contaminated during storage).

[13] See, in particular, section 75 Criminal Justice Act 2003. In modern times the double jeopardy rule has often been discussed in the same breath as the Stephen Lawrence case (1994), that became a *cause célèbre* after four white young men were acquitted of his allegedly racist murder. This led to the MacPherson Report (1999; Cm 4262) that criticised the MPS re its investigation, including for institutional racism. MacPherson recommended that the double jeopardy rule be re-considered. Allegations were being made that the acquittals represented a miscarriage of justice.

[14] It is the largest anywhere: 5.2 per cent of the UK population is on it as against 0.5 per cent in the USA. In the UK it now contains 'most of the known criminal population'. (Both statements made by PITO).

December 2005 when the FSS was privatised. A National DNA-database annual report has been produced each year since 2002.

Some DNA issues

Questions have been raised as to why so many people who have been arrested but not convicted of any offence remain on the database. Before 2001, the police could take DNA samples during investigations but had to destroy these and the records derived from them if the people concerned were acquitted or charges were not proceeded with. The law was changed in that year to remove this requirement, and again in 2004 so that DNA samples can now be taken from anyone arrested for a recordable offence and detained in a police station (a relatively low-level condition). The Home Office claims that any intrusion into personal privacy is proportionate to the benefits that are gained by securing convictions and in terms of crime prevention and crime reduction generally; albeit that this has made little impact with those civil liberties and human rights organizations who perceive the emergence of a Big Brother state.[15] There have also been questions about the over-representation of black people and people who are below the age of 18 on the database. But whilst the Home Office accepts that people under 18 account for 23 per cent of all arrests, it also asserts that a comparative proportion of profiles is to be expected. There are no legal powers to take a DNA sample from anyone under ten years of age (the UK age of criminal responsibility) without the consent of a parent or guardian. But this, of course, begs the question whether so many young people should be being arrested and it does not bode well for the future as ever larger numbers of young arrestees grow up. Suggestions that there should be an automatic link between the DNA-database and identity cards have been resisted by human rights and civil liberties campaigners who say that they are concerned about the many less legitimate uses to which such data could potentially be diverted.

POLICE SCIENCE AND TECHNOLOGY

Police forces (see, generally, *Chapter 3*) also play their own role in science and technology. Thus, for example:

- investigating officers use forensic science in a bid to more accurately detect crime, obtain convictions or clear people;

---

[15] By the end of 2005, some 200,000 samples had been retained that would have been destroyed pre the 2001 changes: 8,000 of these matched with DNA taken from crime scenes, involving nearly 14,000 offences, including murders and rapes. (Home Office)

- hi-tech communications and information systems enable officers to spend more time engaging with people and less time tied up with time-consuming manual tasks;[16]
- leading-edge science and technology is being used to combat organized crime and terrorism; and
- the police are using a range of sophisticated information or communications technology, forensic science and similar advances.

There is a Police National Computer (PNC) that has evolved into a sophisticated intelligence tool that holds considerable amounts of data on offenders, vehicles and property, and that can now be accessed in seconds via over 30,000 terminals in the UK. In addition to the National DNA-database (above), there is also one for fingerprints. Another, linked to the Driver and Vehicle Licensing Authority (DVLA) in Swansea seeks to curb traffic offences as do modern breath analysis devices, enforcement cameras, immobilisation, traffic signal and speed measuring devices. A 200-strong team of scientists and engineers work for the Home Office Scientific Development Branch (formerly the Police Scientific Development Branch) to pioneer new ways of combatting crime and similar threats. The Police Science and Technology Strategy is a five-year plan to address technological and scientific needs in police forces. It was presented for the first time in 2003 and has already reached several significant milestones including:

- expansion of the national DNA database (above);
- national rollout of Airwave: a new digital police radio communications service;
- extensive use of Automatic Number Plate Recognition;
- trialling the IMPACT Nominal Index (INI): a database used to check applicants for police contracts and employment for custody, intelligence, domestic violence, crime, firearms and other police-related involvement;
- work towards secure internet portal which would enable;
  —online shared access to case information by criminal justice agencies; and
  —victims of crime to track their cases.[17]

---

[16] Including 'paperwork': always the bane of police officers' lives but now being superseded by modern, electronic recording systems.

[17] Various former responsibilities of the Home Office with regard to victims of crime were transferred to the MOJ in 2007; albeit that the Home Office retains an obvious and shared interest in victims due to its general crime prevention, etc. responsibilities and involvement in raising standards generally and improving police practice.

ANIMAL TESTING

In response to the claims of 'animal activists'[18] and other campaigners, the Home Office has asserted that the development of drugs and medical technologies that help to reduce suffering among humans and animals depends on the carefully regulated use of animals for research. Hence it:

> respect[s] the fact that people have strong ethical objections to the use of animals in scientific procedures. [It has] legislated so experimentation is only permitted when there is no alternative research technique and the expected benefits outweigh any possible adverse effects.

But the Home Office is expressly determined to confront animal rights extremism by:

> ensuring that lawful and properly conducted research and business can take place freely in the UK by ending the threat of unlawful disruption and intimidation by animal rights extremists and deterring and prosecuting animal rights extremists so that they no longer pose a threat from unlawful direct action.[19]

The Home Office also claims to have reduced the number of experiments involving live animals by half over the last 30 years by: developing new techniques (e.g. that enable testing of new drugs against fever-causing agents using human blood cells instead of rabbits); and introducing rigorous standards stipulating that animal tests cannot be conducted when there is a validated alternative method. Both the breeding and supply of animals for use in scientific procedures is regulated in the UK by the Animals (Scientific Procedures) Act 1986.[20] Proposals to use animals in scientific projects are individually scrutinised and licences only granted by the Home Office when certain criteria to avoid animal suffering are met. Animal laboratories must adhere to a code of practice and are monitored by trained officers who make unannounced inspections.

Oversight and advice
The Animals in Scientific Procedures Inspectorate (ASP) provides scientific advice to the home secretary and to the officials who operate the system of

---

[18] Also, nowadays, sometimes called 'terrorists': see, generally, *Chapter 5*. High profile events include the actions and imprisonment of activists re Huntingdon Life Sciences and Oxford University, and the desecration of a woman's grave in Staffordshire when her corpse was held to ransom, leading to the closure of a large guinea-pig farm. New legislation targets the making of secondary threats, e.g. to suppliers and contractors; that was triggered by the activities of the quasi-terrorist Animal Liberation Front (ALF).

[19] For further information, see the National Extremism Tactical Coordination Unit (NETCU) website at www.netcu.org.uk

[20] See, also, the various regulations concerning such matters made under the 1986 Act.

licences approval for laboratories. There is also an Animal Procedures Committee (APC) to advise on matters relating to any scientific procedures which could cause an animal pain, suffering, distress or permanent harm.

DRUGS AND DRUG-TESTING

There is within the Home Office a Crime and Drug Strategy Directorate that *in toto* comprises the following units (alphabetically):

- Anti-social Behaviour and Alcohol Unit;
- Crime and Drugs Legislation and Enforcement Unit;
- Crime and Drugs Research Analysis;
- Crime and Drugs Resources Unit;
- Crime Strategy Unit;
- Drugs Strategy Unit; and
- Violent Crime Unit.

Drugs are a specialist topic[21] and no cursory treatment can hope to indicate the depth and breadth of the arrangements to police drug crime or to deflect drug users away from addictions, habit and networks that in many instances involve criminal misuse of drugs.[22] Controversially, home secretaries David Blunkett and Dr John Reid were obliged to deal with what might be described as a marker within the UK drugs debate: whether or not cannabis should be downgraded from being a Class B to a Class C drug. First it was downgraded (in 2003), but the debate concerning reversal of that law has continued. Other complex issues concern the legalisation of drugs; punishment versus treatment (or whether to 'medicalise' the problem); whether or not drugs or drug treatment should be paid for by the National Health Service (NHS); and the nature of the many schemes that exist to support or wean away drug-users of various kinds.[23] Drug-related crime has an enormous effect on life in the UK and the black economy; whilst at another extreme, questions of international drug law enforcement merge with hugely difficult geo-political questions about global policies and international relations such as whether to destroy opium crops in Afghanistan.

---

[21] Some suggested sources of information are included in *Appendix IV*.

[22] As to which, see *Misuse of Drugs: A Straightforward Guide to the Law* (2007), Jason-Lloyd, L, Waterside Press.

[23] The debate is also reflected in that concerning alcohol misuse; that is also intertwined with economic issues due to the scale of the (legitimate) drinks industry.

Home Office Drug Strategy Unit
The Drug Strategy Unit is responsible for reducing the availability and abuse of dangerous drugs. It works closely with the Department of Health, the Department for Children, Schools and Families and the Treasury, as well as with key national agencies in the drug field. The unit notes, among other things, that drug misuse can lead to many problems in communities 'from an increase in crime, to under-achievement in education by young people':

> We are working hard to prevent these problems by implementing a range of policies and interventions known as the Drug Strategy. This focuses on the most dangerous drugs and problematic drug users as they cause the most harm to themselves, their families and communities.

Its aims include: preventing drugs misuse; reducing the availability of drugs; reducing drug use and drug-related offending through treatment and support; and reducing drug-related crime. It places the cost of such misuse in terms of government spending alone at £1.5 billion per annum noting that over 10,000 people are employed as 'drug professionals' (up 50 per cent since 2002); and that as an investment in the future, 96 per cent of secondary and 80 per cent of primary schools have now developed drug education policies. It estimates that 20,000 young people become adult problem drug users every year so that the present focus of UK drug misuse policy is on 'encouraging young people to choose not to take illegal drugs'. It also operates a number of initiatives and publications under the banner 'Tackling Drugs, Changing Lives'.

GUNS, KNIVES AND OTHER WEAPONS

Another primary concern of the Home Office is the proliferation of weapons in the UK; as well as issues about whether the police should be armed.[24] Gun and knife crime, particularly amongst young people and with its links to the underworld and organized crime have become a major pre-occupation and indicator of whether or not the UK (or a particular part of it) is a safe place to be. As with drugs, so with violent crime and particularly guns. The Home Office notes vividly their detrimental effects:

> Gun crime kills, maims and intimidates, and is frequently linked to gang activity and the illegal drugs trade in the UK. We are committed to tackling [it] to ensure the safety and security of all British citizens.

---

[24] Repeatedly over the years police rank and file officers have opposed the routine arming of the police, other, e.g. than with CS gas sprays and electronic batons.

But it also points out that contrary to public perception, the overall level of gun crime in the UK is very low, less than 0.5 per cent of all crime recorded by the police; and that in the year ending 31 March 2005 provisional figures showed the use of handguns was down 16 per cent; robberies involving firearms down nine per cent; and serious injuries from firearms offences were down six per cent. But:

> Despite these figures, the number of overall offences involving firearms has been increasing each year since 1997/98. And crime involving imitation weapons was up 55 per cent in 2004-05 compared to the previous year.

Also of concern is a rise in the number of young people carrying real or imitation firearms in an attempt to boost their image, or from a mistaken idea about self-protection. Hence measures such as the introduction of a minimum five-year sentence for people convicted of possessing an illegal firearm; it becoming an offence to possess an air weapon or imitation firearm in public without legal authority or reasonable excuse; an increase in the age limit for possession of air rifles to 17; and the prohibition of certain air weapons that are easily converted to fire live ammunition. The Violent Crime Reduction Act 2006 included measures to target imitation guns (and higher maximum sentences) and tighter standards for manufacturers so that imitation guns cannot be readily converted to fire bullets. The Home Office also seeks to target supplies of firearms including those coming from abroad, via enhanced border controls (*Chapter* 6). It has also established the Connected programme to support local community groups in their fight against gun crime. In 2003, a gun amnesty led to the handing in of 43,908 guns and 1,039,358 rounds of ammunition.

So too knives and 'knife-enabled crime' continue to cause serious harm and create fear in communities. Measures to tackle them include amnesties and best practice guidelines created in conjunction with the Association of Chief Officers of police (ACPO) that:

> ... seek to build on the work already done and reinforce the importance of partnership working in the prevention of crime. At the core of the approaches recommended is the need for our work to be intelligence driven. This joint guidance has been produced to enable forces to access the best practice available and help formulate strategies to reduce knife-enabled crime, thus making neighbourhoods and communities safer. We are pleased to recommend this guidance to all forces.

Associated developments include proposals in the Offender Management and Sentencing Bill (2007) for a violent offender order that police can apply for from a magistrates' court and that might be linked to a Violent Offender Register.[25]

---

[25] Although such proposals have provoked opposition from the Council of Circuit Judges as being overbearing and possibly an affront to human rights.

RESEARCH, DEVELOPMENT AND STATISTICS

The Research, Development and Statistics Directorate of the Home Office (RDS) is dedicated to researching and collecting statistics, including in particular in relation to crime, justice and immigration. With the transfer of certain functions to the MOJ and the prospect of a substantial research operation within that department the RDS may be subject to certain adjustments. Further to this, concerns have arisen about the way that the range of statistics are decided upon and their interpretation and use by government; this being one of the issues that fall under the broad head of 'democratic engagement' that is itself part of a wider debate about constitutional change that has arisen under prime minister Gordon Brown since July 2007. Whatever the integrity of researchers, such suggestions contains within them the implied criticism that research may have been misused, constructed or reinterpreted for political ends. There is also issue about how and what is counted and, e.g. whether like is being compared with like when statements are made to the effect that 'crime is falling'. It appears to be generally agreed that crime *is* falling; that crime generally has fallen by some 35 per cent over the past ten years; and that fear of crime may be out of proportion to the reality of the threat. But commentators are quick to point out that crime is changing, that a relatively small fall in burglary has been more than overtaken by shifts to other forms of maybe largely uncounted new forms of crimes that are occurring on a vast scale (see, especially, *Chapter 7*); or that there is simply a displacement of crime into other areas that do not register in the statistics. Further, violent crime is acknowledged to be rising: something that often appears only in the small print. Other difficulties are explained by RDS itself (below).

The Research, Development and Statistics Directorate (RDS)
RDS is at the heart of such issues and dilemmas. Historically it has provided information, research and statistics on topics that relate to Home Office responsibilities such as crime, the justice system and immigration, including annual, quarterly and monthly *Criminal Statistics* and the separate *British Crime Survey* (BCS) that uses polling methods to asses the views of ordinary people, e.g. about their fear of crime and associated perspectives. The home secretary and other ministers and policy-makers, who need to make decisions based on evidence, rely heavily on RDS research findings to inform their decision-making on policy and strategy and to understand whether these are working or not.

Data is provided by all police forces in England and Wales (*Chapter 3*), who must supply the Home Office with monthly figures for all Crime and Disorder Reduction Partnerships (CDRPs) (*Chapter 4*) in their own area. Publications are then compiled by RDS staff: statisticians, researchers, economists, communications professionals and scientists; all of whom work together to inform Parliament and the general public, as well as their Home Office colleagues. According to the RDS on its web-site:[26]

> An important indicator of police workload, police recorded crime figures provide a good measure of trends in well-reported crimes, and can also be used to analyse local crime patterns ... Police recorded crime figures do not provide the most accurate measure of crime, as they are susceptible to people's reluctance to report some types of crime (such as sexual offences, or those they consider too trivial), and to changes in the way police have been asked to record crime.

And as to the BCS, RDS states:

> The BCS gives a more complete estimate of crime, because it asks people about their actual experiences - thus covering crimes that do not get reported to or recorded by the police. It is also not affected by changes in how police record crime ... As a survey of private households, the BCS is limited to the offences it covers and the victims within its scope, and cannot provide an assessment of crime trends at the local level.

RDS also notes the need for allowances to be made in the statistics for such things as seasonal adjustments; as where there is an influx of visitors to an area at a given time of year; or major events that attract people to the area. Control standards are provided by the Office for National Statistics (ONS), to protect the privacy of individuals who might be identified by the figures in small areas.

There is also a dedicated Drugs Analysis and Research Programme that is the responsibility of an embedded RDS team and undertakes research and analysis for the Home Office Crime and Drug Strategy Directorate (above).

HOME OFFICE WEB-SITES

Another way of assessing the wide remit of the Home Office is the existence of a significant number of Home Office *web-sites* (i.e. in the plural) covering separate aspects of its responsibilities. Links to these, some of which are noted in various footnotes to the individual chapters of this book can be found on main Home Office web-site, www.homeoffice.gov.uk

---

[26] www.homeoffice.gov.uk/rds

The Changed Role
of the Home Secretary

CHAPTER 9

The Changed Role of the Home Secretary

Under the new arrangements described in this book, the home secretary will retain his or her general responsibilities in relation to crime prevention and crime reduction, policing, immigration, threats to internal security, counter-terrorism, organized crime and control of guns, weapons and drugs. He or she will also play a key role vis-à-vis the Government's 'Respect Agenda' and accompanying anti-social behaviour programme (aided by a Home Office Respect Task Force)[1] and Britishness (*Chapter 6*), albeit often now within the shared context of Cabinet Office committees and partnerships of the kind described in earlier chapters. What is likely to change is the sense of dysfunction that formerly stemmed from the Home Office needing to deal with justice-related issues as well: prisoners and people on probation or parole. This may have been great a mis-match to dealing with pressing problems of law and order.

This was perhaps never more evident than when a home secretary was confronting major threats to security on the one hand whilst seeking to encouraging forward-looking initiatives such as restorative justice or 'going straight' on the other. Since May 2007, seemingly, it would be quite in order for a home secretary and the Secretary of State for Justice and Lord Chancellor to have differences of opinion and perspective, given the clear distinction in their roles. But no longer does the home secretary need to cultivate a split personality.

THE ROLE OF THE HOME SECRETARY

The fresh division of responsibilities as between the Home Office and MOJ also relieves the home secretary of troublesome distractions of the kind that led John Reid when home secretary to declare that the Home Office was 'not fit for purpose' (see, further, *Chapter 10*). There is thus a greater opportunity to focus wholeheartedly on public protection, public safety, border controls and law and order. Hopefully, this will lead to better overall coherence, clarity, integrity and responses across the entire Criminal Justice System (CJS). The new-style home secretary, post-September 11, post July 7 (and other London and Glasgow bombings) can become increasingly and legitimately crime, security, public safety, policing and immigration-oriented – his or her primary duty being *to make people feel safe* and as far as is humanly possible *to ensure that they are safe*. This

---

[1]   As noted elsewhere in this book the new Department for Children, Schools and Families will play a forward role in relation to anti-social behaviour and youth justice.

accords with Gordon Brown's statement as incoming prime minister that the first priority of Government is the security of its citizens (*Chapter 1*). The Home Office at its web-site describes the role of the home secretary by saying that he or she 'has overall responsibility for the work of the Home Office:

- crime reduction [*Chapter 4*];
- security [*Chapters 1* and 5 in particular];
- counter-terrorism [*Chapter 5*];
- immigration [*Chapter 6*];
- civil emergencies [*Chapter 5*]; and
- related expenditure issues.'

These functions are discharged through various specialist units and partnership networks as noted in earlier chapters as well as via the powerful influences that he or she exerts by making key speeches, announcements, in giving reports to Parliament and associated activities. The way in which a home secretary does this sets the tone and the temperature for the entire process.

In terms of personal style, he or she can take the lead, set an example, seek to drive events forward on his or her own initiative relying on his or her underlying beliefs and values (and hopefully on the basis of sound information and intelligence). At the opposite extreme, a home secretary, provided that he or she is not over-concerned with reform, can simply respond to pressures. A 'strong' home secretary is perhaps one who responds and reforms whilst at the same time recognising the longstanding values of the Home Office, built up over many years. In modern times, however, there has sometimes been a tendency to be media-conscious, overly-responsive to high profile events and dismissive of expertise or experience, so long as actions register on the political thermometer and in the opinion polls. The political life of a home secretary (or any other politician) is transient – the list at the end of this chapter shows sometimes just how transient - but the Home Office must deal with the longer term effects of any decision taken by its minister – as must, of course, the country.

The scale of the task

Even after the creation of the new Home Office, it might be suggested, no one individual has the capacity to deal with all the minutiae of the role or to comprehend every dynamic and longer term implications of a particular course of action. Hence, e.g. the existence of ministers of state with responsibility (post-July 2007) for various areas of Home Office responsibility; but also officials, leaders of various units, advisors and research and development of the kind described in *Chapter 8*. Whilst the home secretary (and his or her senior officials) is the individual who must face sleepless nights, be available at any time of day or night, chair emergency committees, and take hard and occasionally impossible decisions – as well as answer to Parliament for his or her actions – he or she is assisted by various junior ministers, including, now a minister for security, counter-terrorism and the police; and for immigration and asylum.[2] Home Office officials lead various units and report to the home secretary as noted in *Chapter 4*.

Working together and strengthening links

Post-Home Office split the home secretary and Lord Chancellor have vowed to tackle their individual areas of responsibility by working together to protect the public; and maintaining and strengthening links between the Home Office and the Ministry of Justice (MOJ). In this, as the Home Office notes at its web-site,[3] the National Criminal Justice Board 'will remain a crucial body for bringing the deliverers and the policy-makers together'. So will the Cabinet Office in terms of policy-setting at the highest level. There are delicate and sensitive areas of activity to consider, not least the Lord Chancellor's duty to protect the independence of the judiciary; but in other matters such as the sharing of data about high-risk offenders or the arrangements to ensure that where the police do arrest someone they are dealt with without delay and consistent with other justice-based considerations it is not simply desirable that interdepartmental links exist, but essential. It may have been a failure to work together or communicate properly in the past that led to sometimes convoluted or dysfunctional arrangements and to a lack of confidence in the CJS as a whole.[4]

SOME HISTORICAL BACKGROUND

The origins of the position of home secretary can be traced to the office of King's Secretary and as far back as the 14th century. Seemingly it was not a particularly prestigious or distinguished office at first, but its status and influence rose in Tudor times. Thomas Cromwell (1485-1540) was effectively King Henry VIII's chief minister (and it is interesting that one of the things that he was concerning himself with in 1537 was the organization of local justice, just as many of his successors did from time-to-time thereafter). Certainly, by 1782 with the division of the former sole office of Secretary of State into that for the Home Department and the Foreign Office, the post began to take on some of the signs of its modern-day incarnation. That strategic division of responsibilities took no account of the

---

[2] Former responsibilities for areas such as young people, criminal justice, sentencing, law reform or custodial provision have passed to the MOJ or are shared between ministries.

[3] www.homeoffice.gov.uk

[4] But it might be suggested that for people with no direct stake in the CJS, especially those with an axe to grind there is nothing to lose by undermining or belittling it. There is a difference between informed and 'vexatious'/'tendentious' interpretations of events.

need for justice-related matters to be located elsewhere, which only came with the later transferring out of responsibility to the then Lord Chancellor's Deparment (LCD) and later the Department of Constitutional Affairs (DCA)and MOJ as described in *Chapter 1*. According to David Faulkner, before 1782, the home secretary's functions 'had come to be recognised as:

- providing the main channel of communication between the King and his subjects, including Parliament;
- advice to the King on the exercise of the prerogative of mercy;
- conveying instructions to the King's Officers at home and abroad – usually in earlier times to Lords Lieutenants and sheriffs rather than chief constables, but also to magistrates and local authorities a recognizably the beginning of our present Home Office Circulars.'[5]

And further:

> The secretary of state was in those early days very much the servant of the Crown, and his association with the political parties and his accountability to Parliament only came later, especially after 1688.[6] But it is still worth remembering that the secretary of state and Home Office officials are still first and foremost servants of the Crown, with a duty to the Crown that transcends party political loyalties. Although this duty is not expressed in statute, and it is not always clear how it can be defined or enforced in practice, the notion of an overriding duty to the Crown, which ministers and officials share on equal terms, is one which I personally find helpful in giving some coherence and principle to our job as Home office officials. For practical purposes the official is of course responsible to the political administration of the day.[7]

This passage is doubly interesting in highlighting the fact that the home secretary is a political animal whereas his or her officials are decidedly not (even though they owe the home secretary certain loyalties). No politician should control judicial functions, of course – although someone who is accountable to the electorate must be found to administer them. Faulkner goes on to add that officials may sometimes need to tender advice with which the home secretary may well disagree, but it remains their duty to give it.

By 1782 the party system had become well-established and the secretary of state had become firmly associated with the political administration when the first secretary of state for the Home Department, Lord Shelburne, was appointed.

---

[5] Taken from an unpublished internal Home Office 'Occasional Paper in Administrative Studies', No. 2 of 1991. This can new be viewed at www.watersidepress.co.uk For certain comments about HOCs, see *Chapter 1*.

[6] i.e. with the Glorious Revolution and a constitutional monarchy.

[7] Source as for footnote 3.

It is not long thereafter that the department began its expansion as it wrestled with the creation of penal colonies abroad, the Napoleonic Wars and their aftermath as soldiers returned to unemployment in the UK and introducing legislation for Britain's earliest police forces. It was also at this point that the home secretary's role began to focus on the police, prisons and immigration.

A poisoned challice?

The office of home secretary has attracted a various of epithets across the years along the lines of 'political graveyard' or 'poisoned chalice'. The Home Office is a place where politicians may sacrifice their career to random, possibly unforeseeable or wholly uncontrollable events with regard to which the political democratic process ultimately calls for their heads. Conversely, a cynic might suggest that the 'strength', 'boldness' or 'toughness' of a home secretary (all qualities that seem to appeal to popular conceptions of what being home secretary is about), may fall to be judged by favourable outcomes or responses. Some favourable outcomes may be equally fortuitous.[8] But these are matters for students of human nature and fallibility; public safety must be guaranteed whatever the political rules or anthropological observations. Over time, the resolve of a home secretary may have been judged by his or her preparedness to call out the troops or militia to deal with civil disorder, or the power of his or her rhetoric or oratory in support of penal change. A significant number of home secretaries have gone on to higher office.[9]

DIVERSE APPROACHES TO THE ROLE

It would be impossible here to fully outline the potential for differences of approach - but it is possible to give a flavour of the way in which the role of home secretary has changed via snapshots of people who have held that post. First, two politics giants who not only survived the 'graveyard' reputation of the role but went on to serve as prime minister.

Viscount Sidmouth

Viscount Sidmouth (formerly Henry Addington) (1757-1844) is frequently represented as one of the most repressive incumbents, someone given to aggressive tactics including his reliance on the militia. Elected as Tory member of

---

[8] Historically, an acid test was his or her readiness to allow justice to take its course and the death sentence to be carried out, as against any views on this expressed at the time.

[9] Including Viscount Sidmouth and Winston Churchill (see text) as well as, e.g. Sir Robert Peel, Viscount Palmerston, Gwilym Lloyd Geord and James Callaghan. Tony Blair was shadow spokesman for Home Affairs. Uniquely, it seems, Viscount Sidmouth was prime minister (1801–1804) before becoming Home Secretary (1812–1822).

Parliament for Devizes, Wiltshire in 1784 and one-time Speaker of the House of Commons (when he was involved in the impeachment of Warren Hastings and renowned *inter alia* for his opposition to Catholic emancipation) he became home secretary in Lord Liverpool's administration, a post that he held for ten years from 1812-1822, at a time of economic depression and social unrest. His responses included the suspension of *habeas corpus* (1817), reviving laws against seditious meetings, setting up a network of secret informers known as 'Sidmouth's spies', and issuing 'instructions' to Lords Lieutenants and local magistrates to crack down on given offences, including blasphemy and the then criminal offence of seditious libel. It is alleged that he also sought to constrain the discretion of judges and magistrates and took a controlling stance vis-à-vis policing and to the extent that he could, decisions of the courts. His actions were partially responsible for provoking the Peterloo Massacre; and one of his responses was a highly repressive sequence of legislation known as the Six Acts.

Winston Churchill

Winston Leonard Spencer Churchill (later Sir Winston) (1874-1965) was home secretary under the Liberal Government from 1910-1911. In one speech about imprisonment in the House of Commons[10] he pressed for improvements in prison conditions, shorter sentences, sentencing guidelines and alternatives to custody. Famously he actively took part alongside the police on the street in the Siege of Sydney Street in 1912, an early terrorist threat involving offenders from Eastern Europe. Nonetheless, he also courted controversy by making using use of the militia to quell riots, including at Tonypandy, South Wales. Famously, he asserted that:

> The mood and temper of the public in regard to the treatment of crime and criminals is one of the most unfailing tests of the civilisation of any country.

More generally, he argued for calm, dispassionate recognition of the rights of an accused with regard to the actions of the state and for constant 'heart-searching' by all people concerned with punishment, together with an eagerness for rehabilitation once offenders had 'paid their dues'. There should, Churchill argued, be tireless efforts to discover curative and regenerative processes, claiming that 'there is a treasure, if you can only find it, in the heart of every man'. Such attitudes he saw as the mark, measure and stored-up strength of a nation: symbols and proof of its 'living virtue'.[11]

---

[10] 20 July 1910.

[11] Views said to have been affected by a short period spent as a prisoner of war. It emerged in 2007 that in the late-1940s Churchill rejected quotas to curb UK immigration from the Commonwealth (*Chapter 6*) as politically inexpedient.

Modern times

The Labour home secretary Roy Jenkins is sometimes described, especially by penal reformers, as 'the only liberal home secretary'. During his relatively short time in office (1965-6) he set in train various liberal-minded reforms in relations to abortion, homosexuality and theatre censorship[12]. Taking Jenkins as marking the beginning of an era of change, David Faulkner explains how a then new-style of doing business impacted on Home Office officials and how they should respond to the pressure that stem from the political milieu in which, by definition, government officials are obliged to work:

> Perhaps from Roy Jenkins's first period as home secretary, Home Office ministers have become much more active as they themselves had to respond to increasing Parliamentary and other pressure. It is our job to support them in responding to those pressures, whilst stopping short of involving ourselves in party political activity; we must not engage in any public activity in which we know they would disapprove of; and if we think they might but ought not to disapprove, we should obtain their clearance in advance. But the official's relationship with ministers is emphatically not one of passive obedience. It is not the official's job to give ministers the advice they want to hear, but to make sure that the financial, practical and other consequences of a course of action have been properly worked out, and are firmly in minister's minds, before a decision is taken. It is a serious professional failure on our part if we are unprepared or so anxious to please that we fail to provide properly thought out judgement or advice. The other side of the relationship is that ministers should respect and expect that advice, even if they decide not to accept it. If that happens it is the duty of officials to give effect to the decision unless they can be moved to other work or in an extreme case they are prepared to resign.[13]

Faulkner also points to other pressures and dilemmas that would appear to stem chiefly from the changing nature of the role of home secretary and that call for an understanding of values and principles that subsist over time.

Growing politicisation of the role

Other relatively liberal-minded home secretaries of modern times are Douglas Hurd (1985-89) (later Lord Hurd and president of the Prison Reform Trust) and William Whitelaw (1979-83) (both Tories under prime minister Margaret Thatcher). Kenneth Clarke (1992-93) was home secretary at the time of an infamous criminal justice U-turn that saw key parts of the recently implemented and reforming Criminal Justice Act 1991 reversed. It is with Clarke's successor, Michael Howard (1993-7) and his populist slogan 'prison works' that an

---

[12] Jenkins may have been well-suited to the then 'permissive society'.

[13] Taken from an unpublished internal Home Office 'Occasional Paper in Administrative Studies', No2 of 1991. This can new be viewed at www.watersidepress.co.uk

acceleration in the politicisation of criminal justice is mostly associated,[14] fuelled by a media that was becoming increasingly hostile to anything that hinted at tolerance, leniency, understanding or open-mindedness – and all too ready, perhaps, to encourage fundamental change.[15] Since that time, law and order has become a key priority of all political parties: and, whether this should have been the case or not, the ground on which much public debate has been focused.

Soon afterwards, the New Labour Government, led by prime minister Tony Blair, took up office in 1997. It introduced the Human Rights Act 1998 so as to incorporate the European Convention On Human Rights (ECHR), under the banner 'Bringing Rights Home'. Yet, before long, Labour home secretaries were complaining that it inhibited their increasingly punitive and controlling agenda. David Blunkett (home secretary from 2001-2004)[16] who resigned (for personal rather than political reasons) clashed with the judiciary on human rights, something that continued under Dr John Reid (2006-7), these issues going to the roots of judicial independence. At one point Dr Reid's comments on sentences passed by judges had to be 'reinterpreted' by Lord Falconer, the then Lord Chancellor, in ways that more correctly nuanced the differing roles and responsibilities of the home secretary and the judges. It was Dr Reid's revelatory 'not fit for purpose' moment that ultimately led to the Home Office split and the patently more legitimate constitutional re-arrangement described in *Chapter 1*.[17]

THE CONTINUING NEED FOR SAFEGUARDS

In constitutional terms there is a more than purely cosmetic need for a home secretary who understands fundamental values and their underlying rationale. 'Working together', partnership, interdepartmental committees such as those of the Cabinet Office and the strengthening of links across a joined-up criminal justice process all demand the highest standards of integrity with regard to roles, functions and what is known as the separation of powers.[18]. Those of a radical persuasion might suggest that a home secretary driven by media spin and hostility towards the judiciary represents a greater ill than the cures that he or

---

[14] A slogan originating by way of an anwer to those criminologists who argued that 'nothing works'. Notoriously, Michael Howard also declined to take responsibility for an operational matter, the escape of three high security prisoners from Parkhurst Prison on the Isle of Wight, ultimately leading to the dismissal by him of Derek Lewis, the first director general of HM Prison Service to be appointed from the private sector.

[15] Often to longstanding rules of a fundamental nature that might, e.g. be entrenched in any written constitution, such as the right to silence and some golden rules of evidence.

[16] So far as is known, the UK's first blind minister of state.

[17] See, also, *Chapter 10* for more information about how that split came about.

[18] As to which see the companion to this work, *The New Ministry of Justice*.

she is propounding. It risks long term damage to the checks, balances and safeguards that underpin democracy.

At first sight, the events of 2007 – which coincided with the appointment of the first woman Home Secretary, Jacqui Smith – offer encouragement that such principles will be seen as important and worthy of preservation. Incoming prime minister, Gordon Brown has announced his intention to ensure democratic engagement and the involvement of people and communities of all kinds in the democratic process. Further to this there is talk of a new and possibly a written constitution that among other things would unavoidably need to deal with issues of the kind noted above. Anecdotally, there has also been a change of tone, leading to a sense of balance, an indication that the step-change that is represented by the Home Office split may not simply be a reflection of the mechanics of change. Among other things the new arrangements are designed to restore confidence. It is early days, but there would already seem to be a general sense that events are about to enter the fresh era described in *Chapter 10*.

LIST OF BRITISH HOME SECRETARIES SINCE 1794

1794	Duke of Portland		1911	Reginald McKenna
1801	Lord Pelham		1915	Sir John Simon
1803	Charles Yorke		1916	Sir Herbert Samuel
1804	Lord Hawkesbury		1919	Edward Shortt
1806	Earl Spencer		1922	W C Bridgeman
1807	Lord Hawkesbury		1924	Sir William Joynson-Hicks
1808	Lord Liverpool		1929	John R Clynes
1809	Richard Ryder		1931	Sir Herbert Samuel
1812	Viscount Sidmouth		1932	Walter Elliot
1822	Robert Peel		1935	Sir John Simon
1827	William Sturgess Brown		1937	Sir Samuel Hoare
1827	Marquis of Landsdowne		1939	Sir John Anderson
1828	Robert Peel		1940	Herbert Morrison
1830	Viscount Melbourne		1945	Sir Donald Somervell
1834	Viscount Duncannon		1945	James Chuter Ede
1834	Henry Goulburn		1951	Sir David Maxwell Fyfe
1835	Lord John Russell		1954	Gwilym Lloyd George
1839	Marquis of Normanby		1957	Richard A ('Rab') Butler
1841	Sir James Graham		1962	Henry Brooke
1846	Sir George Grey		1964	Sir Frank Soskice
1852	Spencer Walpole		1965	Roy Jenkins
1852	Viscount Palmerston		1967	James Callaghan
1859	Thomas Sotheron-Escourt		1970	Reginald Maudling
1859	Sir George Cornewall-Lewis		1972	Robert Carr
1861	Sir George Grey		1974	Roy Jenkins
1866	Spencer Walpole		1976	Merlyn Rees
1867	Gathorne Hardy		1979	William Whitelaw
1868	Henry A Bruce		1983	Leon Brittan
1873	Robert Lowe		1985	Douglas Hurd
1874	Richard A Cross		1989	David Waddington
1880	Sir William Vernon Harcourt		1991	Kenneth Baker
1885	Sir Richard A Cross		1992	Kenneth Clarke
1886	Hugh E Childers		1993	Michael Howard
1886	HenryMatthews		1997	Jack Straw
1892	Herbert H Asquith		2001	David Blunkett
1895	Sir Matthew White Ridley		2004	Charles Clark
1902	Aretas Akers-Douglas		2006	John Reid
1905	Herbert Gladstone		2007	Jacqui Smith
1910	Winston S Churchill			

The author wishes to acknowledge the work of Brian P Block and John Hostettler on which the earlier part of this list is based.

A Fresh Start and a New Era

CHAPTER 10

A Fresh Start and a New Era

The strategic role and responsibilities of the Home Office and the impact of its still myriad responsibilities permeate the preceding chapters of this book. So do individual aspects of change and development. But it seems that any real understanding of such matters involves a broader knowledge of past events as well as a slightly more prospective view. The former can serve, however superficially in a book of this kind, to locate the new Home Office in an era of considerable political change; the latter to place its responsibilities, tasks and challenges within a world in which everything falls under increasingly close scrutiny and, so we are led to believe, where there are unprecedented threats to public safety and, whether it is correct or not, falling standards in terms of individual behaviour amongst certain sections of society. Neither are crime, punishment, public safety, immigration and other Home Office concerns capable of being filed in tidy compartments; all have a decidedly political dimension.

A CATALYST FOR CHANGE

As noted in *Chapters 1* and *9*, a key trigger for the 2007 changes was the revelation by Dr. John Reid, home secretary, early in 2007 that the Home Office in its then guise was 'not fit for purpose'. Whilst that pronouncement appears to have become a symbolic one it would be wrong to attribute the changes to what may in truth be little more than a media sound-bite. To differing degrees, earlier home secretaries had also found the old Home Office unwieldy and – especially in a post-human rights era – sometimes uncertain in terms of its legitimate boundaries, historic pre-occupations and modern-day priorities. Thus, e.g. for some long time, less attention was paid by the Home Office to the tail end of prison sentences, either in terms of the parole system or recommendations for deportation of foreign national prisoners at the end of their sentences in accordance with the recommendations of judges who had passed sentence. It was perhaps predictable that those things furthest from the commission of an offence, from the victim of a crime or his or her trauma, the least visible to the general public, would be the first to suffer when more high profile threats materialised. The Government had in fact for some time been looking at splitting up the Home Office even if it was not obvious to the casual observer that this was imminent.[1] John Reid's part in this can be read as helping matters along.

More subtle dilemmas

An example of one of the more subtle dilemma facing the Home Office was its close relationship to the Sentencing Guidelines Council (SGC) formed under the Criminal Justice Act 2003;[2] due both to the former rights and duties of the home secretary in relation to the SGC and the physical location of its secretariat in Home Office premises. Maybe this kind of proximity to sentencing was exacerbated by the freedom some home secretaries felt to publicly criticise judges (*Chapter 8*). In several instances, the fault was traceable to the very sentencing law that the Government had itself created. But the wider point is that home secretaries have seen fit to openly criticise judges contrary to an earlier and longstanding convention that ministers do not do so; and that convention is not without a sound constitutional foundation. More importantly still, perhaps, this was against a background in which a whole range of longstanding methods, rules, procedures and ways of conducting judicial and other public affairs had been coming under scrutiny within a programme of sometimes questionable reforms dating back to 1997. The boundaries of what might be permissible were constantly being eroded. Frequently, the views of judges, lawyers and knowledgeable commentators who regarded fundamental principle as important, were being brushed aside. Those who did raise an eyebrow in public were portrayed as out of touch or not dealing with realty.

The case for change

Constitutional, penal and legal reform in the United Kingdom has a long and reputable history. Sometimes reform has been brought about by what were initially radical movements or in response to complaints that the Government, police or other public authorities had acted or responded wrongly or with too heavy a hand. More typically, and especially in modern times, the momentum for reform and progress has been led either by enlightened ministers[3] and their permanent officials, penal reform groups such as the Howard League For Penal Reform, Prison Reform Trust (PRT) or the National Association For the Care and

---

[1] Discussions were already underway in Cabinet committees and the media was on notice that a Ministry of Justice (MOJ) was already under consideration. What caused bemusement is that it should suddenly appear *fait accompli*, following minimal , if any, real consultation with the legal and judicial community: see *The New Ministry of Justice*.

[2] Whereby the home secretary as opposed, post-MOJ, to the Lord Chancellor, had certain rights and duties in terms of direct influence: for a fuller explanation, see the companion volume to this work, *The New Ministry of Justice: An Introduction*.

[3] Some examples of which re home secretaries are noted in *Chapter 9*.

Resettlement of Offenders (Nacro). Occasionally, individuals successfully campaigned for changes in the law. Until the mid-1990s this was a well-established way of proceeding; and, though changes were already underway as described in *Chapter 9*, such issues tended to be dealt with, as far as possible, in a non-politicised way.

After 1997, an existing tendency to introduce new legislation largely as a matter of political judgement, without consultation, often dismissive of expert opinion, advice or the wider debate, began to accelerate. This was accompanied by an increasing volume of legislation affecting crime and punishment; other 'modern' forms of administration across-the-board;[4] and, seemingly, by a corresponding mistrust among the public of Government and politicians in general. The following perceptions of the author of this work may serve as examples of how matters stood by the time that Gordon Brown took over as prime minister soon after the Home Office split and the creation of the MOJ in 2007. There was broad concern:

- across the legal and judicial community that laws were being introduced without adequate or any consultation with stakeholders, even if this was not always openly expressed;
- that an estimated 3,000 new criminal offences had been created, many, in effect, unidentifiable by all but the initiated, stemming from some 60 new Criminal Justice Acts, many only partially implemented, or not at all, making it difficult for judges and practitioners to understand where the law stood at any one moment, not to mention ordinary citizens;
- that experts and experienced practitioners were being relegated to the sidelines in terms of providing background, information, statistics or data, especially if this conflicted with politically-charged agendas;
- there was a growing sense of unease about where the UK as a whole was heading arising from such events as those surrounding the Iraq War and subsequent Hutton inquiry,[5] the role of the attorney general in relation to advice given to the Government re the legality of that war and the secrecy of that and other advice, as well as involvement in prosecution-decision making where the Government might be perceived to have an interest;[6]

---

[4] There has also been constantly changing language and terminology that make things hard to track of or challenge. Some people have referred to this as 'unspeak', a means of dodging democratic accountability, public involvement and transparency.

[5] Concerning the death of the Home Office scientist Dr David Kelly and sources of intelligence.

[6] Principally re the legality of the Iraq War (unpublished), allegations of bribery at BAE systems (where the investigation was abandoned) and the cash for honours investigation (where the Crown Prosecution Service (CPS) ultimately decided against

- about an increase in police powers, ostensibly to deal with terrorism in the wake of the London bombings of 7 July 2005 in particular, but that were perceived by many civil liberties and human rights groups to go beyond what may have been needed or proportionate to the nature of the threat and that were being used in patently 'non-terrorist' situations;[7]
- about regular assertions by Government of a need for increasingly greater powers to deal with terrorism in particular, including of 90 days detention without charge to allow complex investigations to take place – a move that led to the Government's first defeat in the House of Commons since 1997 when that proposal was rejected;
- about government by legislation; a style of administration in which any problematic event or criticism would (might) be followed by (the promise of) a new law;
- that Government was simply seeking powers where these were 'asked for' or 'demanded' by the police, leading also to tensions on occasion about whether the police had asked for particular powers or not;
- about the development or over-use of quasi- criminal powers such as the anti-social behaviour order (ASBO) and the handing (or downgrading) of powers to a range of public authorities or their officials, including by growing use of administrative fixed penalty notices and fines;[8]
- ways the way in which ministers would 'talk tough', defensively, and frequently aggressively concerning any matters on which they were challenged, or that appeared to question their existing strategies, such that democratic engagement was at-risk of becoming dysfunctional and repressed – and confrontation the order of the day;
- concerning high profile cases in which the police appeared to use excessive force when exercising their legitimate – often new and greater – powers which tended to trigger resentment, especially where people from minority ethnic or religious groups were involved as suspects; and
- a general sense that none of this was achieving anything positive.

It would be quite one-sided to pretend that many of the above points do not have 'another side to the story', or that they are not part of a larger debate. But it would be wrong to ignore the sense of unease that seems to have been prevalent

---

prosecution for lack of reliable or other sufficient evidence). In the midst of this, Tony Blair was to suffer the indignity of being the first serving prime minister to be interviewed as a witness in a criminal inquiry (cash for honours).

[7] See, generally *Chapter 5.*

[8] 'Administrative' meaning imposed by an official, as opposed to 'judicial', imposed by a judge or magistrate. Administrative fines may involve a right of appeal to a court but that process is relatively cumbersome. Private sector fines have also burgeoned.

by the time the decision was made to remove various problematic and justice-related areas of responsibility from the Home Office to the MOJ or elsewhere. In a sense, something needed to be done to overcome the sense of malaise that may have been setting in amongst certain officials as well as the general public. That the Home Office split might create an all-embracing solution in itself would seem over-optimistic. But taken alongside a fresh start and a re-assertion of values and principles of the kind noted in earlier chapters of this book there might be some expectations of improvement.[9]

A DANGER OF ISSUE FATIGUE

In 2006, in launching *Rebalancing the Criminal Justice System in Favour of the Law-abiding Majority: Cutting Crime, Reducing Re-offending and Protecting the Public*[10] prime minister Tony Blair and home secretary John Reid jointly announced, a large number of proposals and measures designed to rebalance the Criminal Justice System (CJS). There would, among other things, be a further 8,000 new prison places (on top of 900 extra places already under construction) taking capacity across the existing prison estate to some 80,400 by the autumn 2007. This formed 'the backbone' of a raft of measures focusing on tackling violent and persistent offenders thereby 'putting public protection at the heart of the justice system'. Further proposals included 'tough' new measures to 'crack down' on anti-social behaviour, longer sentences for serious offenders and moves to encourage more clarity and honesty in sentencing. A review would examine among other things the Human Rights Act 1998 to promote what was described as a common-sense balance between the rights of individuals and the rights of the public to be protected against harm. There was even talk of that Act being repealed if it stood in the way of public protection. The statement also promised a four-year maximum penalty for carrying a knife; tougher sentences for violent offenders; that persistent offenders would be subject to restrictions on release from prison; the introduction of a new form of violent offender order; that Parole Board decisions to release prisoners would be unanimous; new tactics for dealing with offenders on drugs; and a drive to return more foreign national prisoners to serve sentences in their home country.

Additionally, victims and communities would be 'put first', offenders would pay more to compensate their victims and the Home Office would ensure that the victims' voice would be heard concerning the release of the most serious offenders. Criminal justice agencies would be required to put public safety at the heart of their work. Automatic sentencing discounts for guilty pleas (described as

---

[9] See, in particular, *Chapter 9*.
[10] Central Office of Information on behalf of the Home Office, July 2006. Ref: 275921.

'time-off') would be ended. So would discounts for offenders who were re-sentenced on appeal. Judges would be allowed more discretion with a view to ending the automatic halving of tariffs for those given indeterminate sentences. There would be tougher enforcement with regard to offenders who breached parole licences and a presumption of custody for offenders who 'jumped bail'. The return to custody of offenders who breached their parole licence would be speeded up; aided by the introduction of a national enforcement service by 2007/2008; and there would be consultation on new powers for probation officers to vary punishments, or police officers to impose them – described as 'simple, speedy, summary justice'. There would be live TV links from police stations to courts to speed up the processing of low-level guilty pleas; an expansion of the use of conditional cautions to allow prosecutors to impose penalties (such as fixed fines or unpaid work) and without the need for accused people to go to court; and bulk processing of regulatory offences such as failure to obtain a TV licence, thus freeing up magistrates' courts time for more serious offences; and judge-only trials in serious fraud cases – as part of a 'thorough audit' of the CJS.

Concurrent announcements included a new Immigration Nationality Directorate (at that time as a 'shadow agency') (but see, now, *Chapter 6*); a performance framework for the National Offender Management Service (NOMS); a National Policing Improvement Agency (NPIA) police leadership assessments and a revised bonus system for senior officers (*Chapter 3*).

The above developments still represent only some of the changes that were being made or announced, or that were already in embryo[11] and may have had a sound basis; but, arguably, to set out such a wide-ranging and mixed agenda in this way was simply adding to the fatigue and the vagaries that practitioners within Criminal Justice System (CJS) were beginning to feel.

'Rebalancing' had been taking place for some years and was in 2006 in danger of becoming a cliché. The 2002 White Paper, *Justice For All*[12] jointly issued by the Lord Chancellor, home secretary and attorney general sought to rebalance the CJS as between victims and offenders. The 2006 paper came on top of an existing heavy agenda of related reforms and in some cases still un-implemented measures such as several of those within the Criminal Justice Act 2003, itself a major restructuring of aspects of criminal justice and sentencing aimed at 'rebalancing'. Few of the 2006 announcements appear to have involved substantial input by practitioners with knowledge of the everyday problems - other perhaps than their complaints that they were already suffering from issue fatigue. Where some of the 'changes' stand today remains a mystery to many people close to events. Even some judges have complained that law and practice has become unintelligible.

---

[11] Which, it seems, that the Home Office split was, behind the scenes: see earlier in the text.
[12] Cm 5563.

A WIND OF CHANGE

Against this background, various key strands of development now combine in a way that may presage a fresh era; with potentially encouraging signs for the future:

- first and most obviously, the change in responsibilities as between the Home Office itself and the MOJ – albeit that this depends on how the Home Office manages its new remit and whether, e.g. the MOJ is able to satisfactorily resolve still outstanding issues around the protection of the independence of the judiciary in particular, matters that may ultimately fall to be resolved in terms of constitutional change;
- second, the momentum for change that was created shortly after the Home Office split by a change of prime minister and moves in the direction of more transparent and open forms of government and democratic accountability, as signalled in particular by a Green Paper, *The Governance of Britain*, issued jointly by the prime minister and Secretary of State for Justice and Lord Chancellor;[13] and
- thirdly, indications of a return to the days when issues of the kind that fall to the Home Office were dealt with by that department in the light of meaningful consultation, including with practitioners, experts, reform groups and others, within processes of a more democratic nature more in line with its traditional and longstanding values.

As already noted in *Chapter 8*, it is early days for any conclusive judgement, but there would seem to be a wind of change that stems at least in part from a backlash against factors of the kind noted earlier in this chapter. In one novel approach, prime minister Gordon Brown made a statement to the House of Commons following Question Time on 25 July 2007 concerning the Government's proposals to deal with terrorism, as noted in *Chapter 5*. Whichever side of the political divide the observer may fall on, it would be difficult not to note the contrast with what the general public had become used to. Similarly, with the new home secretary Jacqui Smith's response to attempted terrorist bombings in Glasgow and London, reproduced in *Appendix II* to this work, that is notable for its lack of direct confrontation or anger.

---

[13] Ministry of Justice (2007); Cm 7170.

Appendix I *Home Office Aims, Objectives and Values*

Our aim is to protect the public and secure our future

The Home Office leads a national effort to protect the public from terror, crime and anti-social behaviour. We secure our borders and welcome legal migrants and visitors. We safeguard identity and citizenship. We help build the security, justice and respect that enables people to prosper in a free and tolerant society.

Our objectives

To protect the public, we focus on seven key objectives:

- help people feel safer in their homes and local communities;
- support visible, responsive and accountable policing;
- protect the public from terrorist attack;
- cut crime, especially violent, drug and alcohol-related crime;
- strengthen our borders, fast track asylum decisions, ensure and enforce compliance with our immigration laws, and boost Britain's economy;
- safeguard people's identity and the privileges of citizenship;
- work with our partners to build an efficient, effective and proportionate criminal justice system;

Our values

The values we developed in consultation with our staff and stakeholders, underpin how we will achieve our objectives, and guide our everyday behaviour:

- we deliver for the public;
- we are professional and innovative;
- we work openly and collaboratively; and
- we treat everyone with respect.[1]

---

[1] Source: www.homeofice.gov.uk

Appendix II *Home Secretary's Statement*

On 2 July 2007, incoming home secretary Jacqui Smith made her first speech in that role to Parliament in the immediate aftermath of a number of failed terrorists attacks in London and a car bomb attack on Glasgow Airport. After stating that investigations into these events were currently the Government's 'top priority'. She went on to say:

> To date, six individuals have been arrested in connection with the events, one at Glasgow Airport, a further two in Glasgow, two in Staffordshire (north of Junction 16 on the M6), and one in Liverpool. One further individual of interest remains in a critical condition in hospital. Searches have already been carried out in at least 19 locations, but as I have already said this is a fast-moving investigation.
>
> I am sure the House will join me in thanking all those involved in the response to these incidents: the ambulance crew whose vigilance potentially averted an attack, the police, particularly the explosives officers who manually disabled the device in the Haymarket and the Security Service. In addition, the response from the public and business community – including staff at airports - has been excellent in support of the police and other emergency services.
>
> I would also like to thank colleagues in Scotland and internationally in the United States and in Europe for their messages of support.
>
> Since Friday morning, the government have held four meetings of COBRA, chaired by the prime minister and myself and attended by ministerial colleagues from key government departments and the police and intelligence agencies. Our priority has been to coordinate the necessary responses to protect the public ….
>
> Turning now to that response underway across the country … The police have substantially stepped up protective security measures including: high visibility patrols, including armed response vehicles; increased use of stop and search powers for vehicles and pedestrians; increased physical protection around airport terminal buildings, including tighter controls on access roads; installation of new barriers, in conjunction with airport operators and the Department for Transport …
>
> As ever, these measures are designed to maximise public safety while minimising disruption to normal life.
>
> Terrorism is a serious threat to us all. We must ensure our resources, capability and legislation support our common endeavour to defend the shared values of this country from terror.
>
> To that end: we have doubled expenditure on counter-terrorism since September 2001. Work as part of the current comprehensive spending review will further assess the expenditure necessary.
>
> We have started a full consultative review of counter-terrorism legislation with a view to a bill later this year. This process will continue. Across government, ministers will work together to oversee the delivery of this complex package of measures.
>
> Let us be clear – terrorists are criminals, whose victims come from all walks of life, communities and religious backgrounds. Terrorists attack the values that are shared by all law-abiding citizens. As a government, as communities, as individuals we

need to ensure that the message of the terrorists is rejected ... I very much welcome the strong messages of condemnation we have heard throughout the weekend from community leaders across the country. It is through our unity that the terrorists will eventually be defeated.

I would also like to express my admiration and thanks to members of the public in this country, in all our communities, for their patience and measured response to these events ... My aim as home secretary is to allow the British public to live their lives as they would wish, within the law. The fact that people have been prepared to go about their lives as normally as possible this weekend sends the strongest message to those who wish to destroy our way of life and our freedoms that we will not be intimidated by terror.

Appendix III *Citizenship and Britishness*

The following extracts are from a speech by Gordon Brown[2] delivered at a seminar on Britishness at the Commonwealth Club, London, on 27 Feb 2007 as referred to in *Chapter 6*:

A few years ago less than half [of the UK population] ... identified closely with being British. But today national identity has become far more important: it is not 46 per cent but 65 per cent - two thirds - who now identify Britishness as important, and recent surveys show that British people feel more patriotic about their country than almost [any] other European country ... One reason is that Britain has a unique history - and what has emerged from the long tidal flows of British history - from the 2,000 years of successive waves of invasion, immigration, assimilation and trading partnerships, from the uniquely rich, open and outward looking culture - is I believe a distinctive set of British values which influence British institutions . . .

[As] a multi-national state, with England, Scotland, Wales and now Northern Ireland we are a country united not so much by race or ethnicity but by shared values that have shaped shared institutions. Indeed, when people are asked what they think is important about being British many say our institutions: from the monarchy and the national anthem to the Church of England, the BBC and our sports teams ... But when people are also asked what they admire about Britain, more usually says it is our values: British tolerance, the British belief in liberty and the British sense of fair play. Even before America said in its constitution it was the land of liberty and erected the Statue of Liberty, I think Britain can lay claim to the idea of liberty.

Out of the necessity of finding a way to live together in a multi-national state came the practice of tolerance, then the pursuit of liberty and the principle of fairness to all. Indeed Britain is a country that not only prides itself in its fairness, tolerance and what George Orwell called decency but - as we have seen in recent debates like that over the Big Brother show[3] - wants to be defined by it, defined by being a tolerant, fair and decent country. And there is a golden thread which runs through British history - that runs from that long-ago day in Runnymede in 1215 when arbitrary power was fully challenged with the Magna Carta, on to the first bill of rights in 1689 where Britain became the first country where parliament asserted power over the king, to the democratic reform acts - throughout the individual standing firm against tyranny and then - an even more generous, expansive view of liberty - the idea of all government accountable to the people, evolving into the exciting idea of empowering citizens to control their own lives.

Just as it was in the name of liberty that in the 1800s Britain led the world in abolishing the slave trade - something we celebrate in 2007 - so too, in the 1940s, in

---

2   At the time, Gordon Brown was still Chancellor of the Exchequer. For the full text, see www.hm-treasury.gov.uk
3   A leading Channel 4 TV show in terms of its audience ratings, in which contestants live together in isolation, they and viewers rejecting 'housemates' one at a time (usually) that in 2006 was at the centre of racist controversy due to remarks by participants.

the name of liberty, Britain stood firm against fascism, which is why I would oppose those who say we should do less to teach that period of our history in our schools. But, woven also into that golden thread of liberty are countless strands of common, continuing endeavour in our villages, towns and cities - the efforts and popular achievements of ordinary men and women, with one sentiment in common - a strong sense of duty.

The Britain of local pride, civic duty, civic society and the public realm. The Britain of thousands of charities, voluntary associations, craft societies but also of churches and faith groups. And the Britain of fairness to every individual we see expressed most of all in Britain's unique national health service, health care free of charge to all who need it, founded not on ability to pay but on need - at the core of British history, the very British ideas of 'active citizenship', 'good neighbour', civic pride and the public realm.

Now for years we didn't think we needed to debate or even think in depth about what it was to be a British citizen. But I think more and more people are recognising not just how important their national identity is to them but how important it is to our country. A strong sense of being British helps unite and unify us; it builds stronger social cohesion among communities. We know that other countries have a strong sense of national purpose, even a sense of their own destiny. And so should we. And it helps us deal with issues as varied as what Britain does in Europe; to issues of managed migration and how we better integrate ethnic minorities. Today we have a citizenship test for newcomers wanting to be citizens - 24 questions on life in the UK that lasts for 45 minutes.

We also have citizenship ceremonies. We will soon have a stronger element teaching us about citizenship in the curriculum. But I believe when there is now so much mobility between nations and countries, when we feel strongly that being a British citizen is something to be proud of, then we should emphasise that British citizenship is about more than a test, more than a ceremony - it is a kind of contract between the citizen and the country, involving rights and responsibilities that will protect and enhance the British way of life.

Citizenship means there are common rules and accepted standards. There is now agreement with the proposition I made some time ago that for new citizens, learning English should be a requirement. New citizens should have an understanding of our history and our culture.

But in any national debate on the future of citizenship it is right to consider asking men and women seeking citizenship to undertake some community work in our country or something akin to that that introduces them to a wider range of institutions and people in our country prior to enjoying the benefits of citizenship.

Like you I'm very proud of being British; proud of British values, proud of what we contribute to the world. And like you I want to make sure that we consider today all that we can do to build an even stronger sense of national purpose which unifies us for the years to come.

Appendix IV *Some Further Reading and Internet Sources*

There is no official history of the Home Office as such, but authoritative accounts of its origins and functions have been written by two of its permanent under-secretaries of state. These are, firstly, *The Home Office*, by Sir Edward Troup (Putnam, 1925) and, secondly, *The Home Office* by Sir Frank Newsam (Allen and Unwin, 1954; second edition 1955).

A great deal has been written about matters for which the Home Office is responsible, and subjects such as criminal law, policing and prisons all have an extensive and constantly expanding literature of their own. Those accounts sometimes describe the way in which the Home Office has dealt with a particular issue, but very little has been written dispassionately from the department's own point of view or about the character of the department as an institution. Home secretaries' biographies or autobiographies provide occasional insights into their own activities while holding that office and often the reasons for the actions they took. But officials who may have spent their working lives in the Home Office, and who may sometimes have formed a deep sense of commitment to it, have left few traces of their own. That is perhaps only to be expected in the culture of reticence which has prevailed throughout the department's existence.

Some impression of the Home Office as it was in the 18th and 19th centuries can be found from the five volumes of Leon Radzinowicz's *History of English Criminal Law* (Volume 5 written with Roger Hood), and there is a glimpse from another perspective in Anthony Trollope's account of a miscarriage of justice in his novel *John Galdigate*. In more recent times, the lectures given to commemorate the department's bicentenary in 1982, published by the Royal Institute of Public Administration as *The Home Office: Perspectives on Policy and Administration*, give a range of impressions from distinguished people who were associated with the Home Office at that time. Paul Rock's *A View from the Shadows* describes his view of the relationships and attitudes of the Home Office and the Canadian Solicitor General's Department towards the pressure for greater recognition of the victims of crime during the 1980s (Clarendon Press, 1990). A few copies of occasional papers written by officials for internal purposes survive in private collections, and one such David Faulkner's *Continuity and Change in the Home Office*, which contains valuable insights concerning Home Office values, principles and conventions has been reproduced at www.WatersidePress.co.uk

David Faulkner's *Crime, State and Citizen: A Field Full of Folk* (Waterside Press, 2001; Second edition 2006) describes many of the events in which the Home Office was involved between 1980 and 2001 from an 'insider's' perspective - that of a formerly high-ranking Home Office civil servant - but the focus is again on the events themselves, rather than the Home Office as such.

Information about the present functions, organisation and activities of the Home Office is available on its web-site www.homeoffice.gov.uk and on various web-sites that can be accessed from it. They include those for passports and immigration, policing and research, development and statistics, and others which cover the reform of the department itself. The *Capability Review* published in July 2006, and various materials on the Home Office and public reform more generally are available on or can be accessed from the Cabinet Office web-site www.cabinetoffice.gov.uk (but the relevant web-sites are constantly being changed). The Cabinet Office website also contains the main statements that were made announcing the decision to divide the Home Office and set up a Ministry of Justice, although these are also repeated elsewhere. Historical material is at www.ndad.nationalarchives.gov.uk/AH/2/detail.html

Several publications that give some insight into the world of policing and police leadership are available from Waterside Press: *Principled Policing: Protecting the Public with Integrity* by John Alderson (1998); *Police Leadership in the 21st Century: Philosophy Doctrine and Developments* by Robert Adlam and Peter Villiers (2003) and *Police Ethics* by Seumus Miller, John Blackler and Andrew Alexander (Second edition and first European edition, 2006).

Index